Your SAFE RETIREMENT Roadmap

Your SAFE RETIREMENT Roadmap

A Powerful Guide to Planning and Living A
Deeply-Fulfilled and Prosperous Retirement

FRANK GUTTA, CPA, PFS

Published by FG Publishers

ISBN (paperback): 978-0-578-32409-8
ISBN (ebook): 978-0-578-30223-2

Book design by Christy Day, Constellation Book Services,
www.constellationbookservices.com

Printed in the United States of America

CONTENTS

FOREWORD

I've been working all my life. As a young boy in Washington, D.C., I remember my first job was helping the ladies in the neighborhood carry groceries to their cars in my little red wagon. I couldn't have been more than six years old. But I treasured those nickels, dimes, and quarters, and the hard work they represented. Later, I had a paper route, worked on poultry farms during the summer in Athens, Georgia, and even sold insurance door-to-door when I was still a young college quarterback at the University of Georgia.

When I was drafted by the Minnesota Vikings in 1961, my salary was just $12,500 a year. Can you imagine, compared to the salaries of today's NFL stars? So, I worked every offseason; for Wilson Trucking Systems in North Dakota, giving speeches at local Rotary Clubs and churches, and eventually learning to start and build my own successful businesses, which I am still doing to this day. Not to mention my 18-year 'day job' as starting quarterback of the New York Giants and Minnesota Vikings, where I led my teams to appearances in 3 of the first 11 Super Bowls!

Through it all, I've learned the value of hard work, the pride of earning a paycheck, and the challenges (and thrills) of building and running a business. It takes a great level of commitment to work hard to create your success. If you're reading this book, I'd venture that you've had similar experiences and share a similar work ethic. You've poured years of hard work into building your career or your business, into raising a family, into creating a legacy. Now, you're approaching (or perhaps already in) retirement. A chance to enjoy travel, grandkids, hobbies, or whatever you like. Maybe a chance to turn a lifelong passion into a second career, or to get active supporting a cause. In short, to live a ***fulfilled*** retirement.

But to do all those things, you must have a plan. To quote a famous business leader: "An idiot *with* a plan will beat a genius *without* a plan." The roadblocks facing a successful retirement today are all too real. We are living longer than previous generations ever dreamed, few of us have guaranteed pensions anymore, and we face the perpetual uncertainties of stock market downturns, rising inflation, taxes, and more. To enjoy the retirement that we've dreamed of, we must have a plan to protect what we've built and make it last.

When I learned that Frank Gutta had written this book, I was thrilled to contribute this foreword. I have known and worked closely with Frank for more than 15 years. When I started Tarkenton Financial in 2003, I set out to build a network of like-minded financial professionals who were as passionate as I was about helping people in or near retirement. Frank fits the bill. As one of my top representatives with Tarkenton Financial, Frank has those values and work ethic I mentioned earlier, and he has shown a commitment to providing every single client with the education, tools, and honest guidance needed to make informed decisions about retirement. Frank has helped hundreds of people create a more secure retirement using his careful planning approach and his four-bucket system.

At 81 years old, I still wake up every day fulfilled and full of energy, ready to take on what the day brings. I work because I *choose* to, not because I *have* to. Retirement security is a great feeling. Thanks for reading this book. It's my hope that the lessons Frank shares will help you create the financial security to go out and live your retirement to the fullest!

Fran Tarkenton
Pro Football Hall of Fame '86
Founder & CEO, Tarkenton Financial

INTRODUCTION

Are you asking yourself **"Will I ever be able to retire?"** You are not alone. Tens of millions of Americans are asking themselves that very same question.

There are even bright young people in their twenties who are asking themselves that question , **"Will Social Security still be around to help me when it is time for me to retire?"**

For Americans aged fifty-five and over, the question "Will I ever be able to retire?" has a special urgency. That question can even be frightening.

If you are already retired, like millions of other retirees, you are probably asking yourself, **"How long will my money last in retirement?"**As you know, due to medical breakthroughs and people taking better care of their health, people are living longer and longer. Many people will live 30 years or longer after retirement.

Do you have the savings and investments needed to pay for all of your living expenses and medical expenses for another 30 years or longer?

As the picture shows, the clock is ticking. The time to get

prepared to live a wonderful, financially secure retirement is NOW.

How to prepare now to live a happy and financially secure retirement is what this book is all about.

Unless your family is blessed to have a lot of cash or financial assets (stocks, mutual funds, annuities, bonds, etc.) or unless you have inherited financial assets or have a large pension or retirement plan, you need to develop a plan now to have the cash and assets you will need to enjoy a worry-free retirement in the future.

There is the proper way and the not-so-proper way of planning for your retirement, as with anything else in life. Perhaps the worst plan of all is to have no plan. I know that it can be challenging to try to develop a comprehensive financial plan on your own. In this book, you will learn how to start working on your financial plan that will enable you and your spouse or significant other to live the retirement you have always dreamed of.

First and foremost, **you need to use good judgment to reduce unnecessary spending, to save money on your taxes, to save more money and to make wise investments.**

If you are not sure about how to go about making the proper

choices, speak to a skilled and experienced financial professional. Do not make choices on your own unless you are an expert in that area.

Your retirement and your future financial security are much too important to leave to chance or guesswork.

A perfect storm has hit people who are currently planning for retirement. According to **Wikipedia**, a perfect storm is "**an event in which a rare combination of circumstances drastically aggravates the event.**"

In this case, the combination of circumstances that are making achieving a financially secure retirement more difficult than ever are: more people living longer than ever, their living expenses are higher than ever and fewer and fewer people today have pension plans.

On top of all of that, banks are paying record low interest rates. According to **Bankrate.com**, in 1981, you could earn 18.3% on some 3-month Certificates of Deposit (C.D.s). As I am writing this in 2021, Bankrate.com says that just about the highest C.D. rate you can earn today on a 3-month C.D. is only 0.4%. That is a decline of 17.9%.

If you had **$500,000 in 1981**, you could earn approximately **$90,000 a year in interest,** which was more than enough for many retirees to live on (especially when combined with Social Security).

Today, with that same $500,000 in 3-month C.D.s, about the most you could earn in interest is $2,000 for an entire year, which is not nearly enough income for anyone to retire.

It is estimated that Boomers today have a collective shortfall of $4.6 billion in terms of what is needed to live comfortably in retirement. One of the accomplishments of which I am most proud is that I have been able to help my clients save millions of dollars in extra funds for their retirement.

Recent research shows that only a small percentage of retirees receive income from a pension plan (https://www.cnbc.com/2020/01/17/heres-where-most-americans-are-really-getting-their-retirement-income.html). The same report shows that a minority of retirees receive income from a 401(k).

I have been a practicing CPA and Personal Financial Specialist for over 35 years. There are more than 650,000 Certified Public accountants in the USA. As you may know, CPAs are the most trusted of all financial advisors.

Of those 650,000+ CPAs, fewer than 6,000 hold the prestigious PFS (Personal Financial Specialist) Designation. I am honored to be in this elite group and I use my expertise to help my clients all over America safely realize their financial dreams.

In this book, you will learn some of the ways I help my clients achieve their financial goals.

THE PASSION THAT DROVE ME TO WRITE THIS BOOK

My uncle worked hard, saved money all his life, and when he was about to retire, he relied on a stockbroker to invest his money with the hope that he could have a reliable income stream during his retirement.

Unfortunately, my uncle retired in 2001 and most of his money was invested in the stock market when the market underwent the horrific crash now known as the dot-com bubble. My uncle lost more than half his portfolio. He had to go back to work just to make ends meet.

How could this happen? It just did not seem right that a good, hard-working man would lose so much of his life's savings so quickly. After witnessing this huge loss, I told myself, "**There has to be a better way.**" I was determined to help educate seniors like my uncle, so this same misfortune would not happen to them.

From my decades of experience as a CPA and retirement planning specialist, I know there is a much better way to take the risk out of stock market investing and tremendously reduce the fear of running out of money. I want seniors to have the **tools, resources, knowledge, and strategies** to not only meet the challenges, but also to enjoy their one and only journey in retirement to the fullest. What you want to do with your money is not as important as the way you want to live your life and how you want to invest in the lives of the people you love. After all, money is nothing but a mixture of cotton and linen printed with ink.

The REAL value of money is what it can do for us and our loved ones, such as enabling us to live the lifestyle we want with dignity and on our own terms.

CHAPTER ONE

POWERFUL EFFECTIVE PLANNING

About fifty years ago, retirement was considered to be the short gap between receiving a gold watch and the last rites.

Happily, retirement today is seen as a long span of time, a whole new life adventure during which we can focus on enjoying life instead of toiling away to earn another dollar.

With the likelihood that we will retire in good health with

many years of retirement in front of us, we now need to carefully plan our retirement years to make sure we get the absolute most out of them.

Whatever your retirement dream—a home in the sun, a boat on a river, a lake, or the ocean, or simply spending time with family, friends and loved ones, traveling, golfing, gardening, enjoying life—almost anything is possible with careful planning.

Have you ever wondered why so many delay or neglect to do retirement planning? With the rush of our daily lives, the demands of raising a family and the pressures of work, it is easy to put off retirement planning until "tomorrow."

Then, all too quickly, millions of Americans find they are on the verge of retirement and it seems it is too late to plan.

Two additional factors that lead so many people to put off retirement planning are lack of knowledge and training.

What is the Solution?

Financial planning for a prosperous retirement is a very complex undertaking. Most people will not have the time, training, or expertise to do this on their own.

Don't be afraid to ask for help. We hire others for a wide variety of tasks ranging from changing the oil in our cars to mowing the lawn to cutting our hair. Almost none of us would ever think of performing our dental work or representing ourselves in court.

We hire professionals to do those tasks because they have the training and expertise to perform those services with a high skill level.

Due to the importance of financial planning in helping us to live and enjoy a long and prosperous retirement, most people should hire a financial professional to help them do this properly.

The great news is that it is now possible to hire some financial professionals at little to no cost. For example, in some cases, the financial professional is paid by the company employing them rather than being paid directly by you.

Reaching our Retirement Income and Lifestyle Goals

To reach your lifestyle goals in retirement, you MUST make sure that you reach your retirement income goals. If you are like most people and lack a sizeable pension or 401(k), how will you reach your retirement income goals? The difference between "almost" reaching your retirement income goals and actually reaching them could mean the difference between living in a small rented apartment during retirement vs. living in your dream house in your dream location.

It could mean the difference between being on a low-quality health insurance plan or having access to the best medical doctors and best hospitals in America.

As you can see, the pay-off from high-quality **retirement income planning** is tremendous.

Reaching your retirement income goals has three key components: You must have the right tools, the right education to know how to use those tools and you MUST avoid large losses from the stock market or real estate along the way to retirement.

Retirement today comes with tremendous opportunities, as well as staggering challenges. These opportunities and challenges stem from the fact that we are living longer and stronger than any generation before us. This should be something we celebrate.

A longer and stronger retirement means that **we can dream bigger dreams, travel to farther places, spend more time with our loved ones and live the lifestyle we truly want to live.**

The challenge that comes with living a long and strong life is: how do we make sure our money lasts as long as we do?

It constantly amazes me that people will spend more time planning a one- or two-week vacation than they will to plan for their retirement, which could last thirty years or more. Today, a sixty-year-old couple has a 40% chance that one of them will live to be ninety-five. So, if you started working at age twenty-five, retired at age sixty, and lived to the age of ninety-five, you could spend as much time in retirement as you did working.

Today, we have GPS in our cars, and I believe that the GPS in mine has actually saved my marriage.

Why do I say that? Because I am one of those guys who never wants to stop to ask for directions and this used to sometimes lead to an argument with my wonderful wife.

Now that we have GPS, I just punch in my destination and by some miracle, I am guided there. But what happens if you punch the wrong address into the GPS? You inevitably end up in the wrong place. This points out the supreme importance of knowing exactly where you want to go.

As important as knowing your destination for planning a trip in your car, it is even more important in retirement planning. After all, if you get a little lost on a car trip, you might lose 30 minutes or less of your time.

If you get lost on your way to your retirement destination, you could lose a huge amount of money or possibly not even be able to retire.

Planning your retirement is one of the most important tasks you have in life. At first, it may seem like a fair amount of work but I am going to share some proven strategies with you in this book.

And, the rich rewards of a well-planned retirement are worth it.

THE POWER OF WRITTEN GOALS

When you think about all of the planning elements for a financially secure retirement, the tasks can seem overwhelming. To simplify everything, start with written goals.

It is not enough to merely think about your retirement. The process of writing your goals down on paper helps to make those goals real.

How do you identify your goals? Start by asking yourself these questions:

1.) WHEN do I want to retire?
2.) How much money or assets do I want to have or accumulate BEFORE I retire?
3.) WHERE do I want to live in retirement? In my current home? Closer to children or grandchildren? In a resort community? Possibly even outside of the United States?
4.) What do I want to do in retirement? What hobbies or recreational interests do I want to pursue? Do I want to travel around the United States or around the world? Do I want to do volunteer work or even start a new career, either part-time or full-time?
5.) WHY do I want to retire? What is my major motivation?

6.) What is on my Bucket List? What am I MOST interested in doing before I am called up to Heaven?
What were my dreams when I was younger? Do I want to fulfill those dreams in retirement or pursue new dreams?

7.) Imagine you retired today and thirty years went by and you looked back and said, **"I loved how I spent those years."** What has to happen now so you can truthfully say that in 30 years?

Developing Your Personal Financial Statement

Most of us have seen or heard about the Financial Statements of corporations and businesses. All serious businesses keep track of their finances.

As important as it is for a business to keep track of its finances, it is just as important for each of us to have a **Personal Financial Statement** as we plan for retirement.

A Personal Financial Statement is an inventory of everything you own and owe. Another way of saying this is that a Personal Financial Statement shows your assets and liabilities.

You will see an example of a Personal Financial Statement on the next page of someone with approximately $2.5 million in assets.

I work with and I can help people with far less in assets than this and I also have clients who have a much larger net worth. I do not judge people based on their income or their assets.

I am trained and motivated to help people in all walks of life and to help people enjoy a safe and financially secure retirement. I do this regardless of their income or assets. I strive to help as many people as I can achieve their retirement goals.

The Personal Financial Statement below will enable you to see the resources you have that can potentially produce income for you in retirement.

Sample Personal Financial Statement as of 12/31/XX

ASSETS (A)	
Cash in Banks	$100,000
Stocks and Bonds	$400,000
Annuities	$250,000
IRAs	$100,000
401k	$275,000
REAL ESTATE	
Primary Home	$750,000
Investment Properties	$500,000
OTHER ASSETS	
Cash Value in Life Insurance	$50,000
Furnishings & Personal Effects	$75,000
Jewelry and Art	$25,000
TOTAL ASSETS	**$2,525,000**
LIABILITIES (B)	
Credit Payable	$2,500
Loans Payable	$15,000
Mortgage—Home	$250,000
Mortgage—Investment Property	$150,000
TOTAL LIABILITIES	**$417,500**
Deferred Income Tax	$200,000
NET WORTH (C)	**$1,907,500**
TOTAL LIABILITIES & NET WORTH	**$2,525,000**

A-This is the total of everything you own as of 12/31/XX.
B-This is a total of all the money you owe as of 12/31/XX.
C-This is the difference between your Assets and Liabilities, which equals your Net Worth

First, review your Assets with a trusted financial advisor. Ask, "Are my assets safe from a stock market crash or real estate crash? How can I protect MORE of my assets and protect MORE of my net worth?"

Next, review ALL of your sources of Investment Income: income from bank accounts, income from annuities, stock dividends, bond interest, real estate rental income, etc. Ask your financial advisor, "Is there a way I can generate MORE income and SAFER income from these investments or alternative investments?"

Next, look at your other sources of income: your job, pension income, Social Security income, etc. Brainstorm ways you can increase this income with your financial advisor.

By doing the above analyses, you know the sources and the total amount of income you have coming in. You now need to determine your expenses—where your money is going.

Working with your financial advisor, brainstorm ideas to lower these expenses without cutting the quality of your life. Yes, it can be done.

Most people who don't have a budget do not know all the ways that money is slipping through their fingers every month. A skilled financial advisor can show you some easy ways to keep track of where your money is going and can show you how to painlessly cut expenses, cut out the fat and eliminate waste.

Remember that you can only manage what you can measure. If you are not keeping track of how much money is coming in and from where—and how much money is going out and for what reasons—you cannot create a wealth-building system.

To get to your financial destination—a happy and prosperous retirement—you need to know WHERE you are now. This points out the supreme importance of having an accurate Personal Financial Statement.

This will be the starting point on the roadmap from where you are now to where you want to be in the future, given the resources you currently have. What adjustments or changes do you need to make so that you can realistically achieve your financial goals? This is the question that a skilled financial advisor can help you answer.

Something that you can do on your own is to gather the data to plug into your Personal Financial Statement.

On the next two pages, you will see a sample Current Monthly and Annual Cash Flow Analysis and a Monthly and Annual Cash Flow Analysis for when you are retired.

Notice the differences between the two. With **current** cash flow, **you are able to save $7,100 per year.**

Your projected **Retirement Cash Flow** shows you need to bring in an extra $15,600 beyond what is currently estimated to be your retirement income.

If you start working with a skilled financial advisor today, there is a high likelihood that you will be able to fill that gap and have all the money you need to live the retirement of your dreams.

Sample Cash Flow Currently

	Monthly	Annually
Mortgage/Rent	$2000	$24000
Utilities	200	2400
Food	500	6000
Entertainment	250	3000
Auto	400	4800
Insurance	250	3000
Maintenance	200	2400
Travel/Vacation	200	2400
House Taxes	250	3000
Taxes	1000	12000
Clothing	100	1200
Retirement Cont.	200	2400
Personal Care	150	1800
Gifts	25	300
Contributions	100	1200
Other	250	3000
TOTAL	**6075**	**$72900**
INCOME		**$80,000**
NET SAVINGS PER YEAR		**$ 7,100**

Sample Cash Flow in Retirement

	Monthly	Annually
Mortgage	0	0
Utilities	$200	$2,400
Food	500	6,000
Auto	250	3,000
Insurance	400	4,800
Maintenance	200	2,400
Taxes	500	6,000
Clothing	200	2,400
Property Taxes	300	3,600
Personal Care	200	2,400
Other	250	3,000
TOTAL	**$3,000**	**$36,000**
Income Social Security	2,500	30,000
Net Savings per Year/Shortfall		-6,000
DISCRETIONARY EXPENSES		
Entertainment	500	6,000
Travel/Vacation	300	3,600
NET SAVINGS/SHORTFALL AFTER ALL EXPENSES	**($1,300)**	**($15,600)**
INCOME NEEDED TO COVER SHORTFALL	**$1,300**	**$15,600**

CHAPTER TWO

MY POWERFUL FOUR-BUCKET SYSTEM

When our parents and grandparents retired, many of them had pensions which gave them a reliable income stream that lasted their lifetime. Today, however, less than 20% of working people have a pension, so the rest of us have to depend on our savings, Social Security, and assets to collect income in retirement.

When the previous generation retired, many people collected the majority of their retirement income from their pension. Social Security was more of a sweetener.

Today, most retirees have to rely upon Social Security as the major source of their retirement income.

If you know you are not going to get a pension in your retirement, what can you do to protect yourself? **Start working today with a skilled financial advisor to create your personal pension plan.**

You do NOT need to rely upon a company or upon the government to create a pension plan—you can do this for yourself.

HOW TO CREATE YOUR PERSONAL PENSION PLAN

You can create your own Personal Pension Plan with what I call **My Powerful Four-Bucket System**.

Your First Bucket

This is your **emergency bucket**. Your emergency funds will be in this bucket. Why do you need emergency funds?

You need them because emergencies always happen—and usually at the most inopportune time. Emergencies can be anything from paying for sudden healthcare costs to unforeseen car troubles. Hundreds of other circumstances can lead to emergencies AND the need for emergency funds.

Emergency funds need to be liquid and easy to access. That means you need to fill this bucket with funds you can get your hands on quickly.

Even though interest rates are currently very low, you still need to keep some money in a checking account or another very liquid account. Sometimes, if you can't quickly get your hands on the cash you need, you cannot get the car repair, appliance repair, food, medicine, medical care or something else you need NOW.

In some cases, if you cannot get the cash you need to pay a bill or get services you need now, a small bill can turn into a much larger bill.

You never want a short-term emergency to affect your long-term goals. You never want a short-term emergency to turn into a longer-term problem because you didn't have the cash needed to deal with the problem when it was small. I usually advise my clients to keep three to six months of living expenses in Bucket Number 1, their Emergency Fund Bucket. Each person and each family are different, and you need customized advice. Therefore, you should consult with a trusted financial advisor to determine the size of the emergency fund reserve that is best for you and your family.

BUCKET #1:
Liquidity because emergencies happen

A Cash Emergency Account has value to help deal with the unexpected things that happen in life. Sometimes the unexpected is good (such as paying for a child's wedding), and sometimes it is not (such as paying for health care costs). A short-term emergency fund can also have the potential value of allowing our long-term money to remain long term.

Your Second Bucket

This is your **long-term growth bucket**. The investments in this bucket enable you to keep up with inflation and, in many cases, to far exceed inflation and to grow your money.

In your second bucket, your investment options could be stocks, mutual funds, ETFs (exchange trade funds), bonds, real estate, and annuities, etc. If well-selected, each of these will grow over time.

You want to make selections based on your risk tolerance. An investment may look very tempting. However, if you do not understand an investment or if it will cause you to lose sleep at night, you should avoid it.

Inflation is known as the silent killer of wealth. Inflation promises that what you buy today will be more expensive in the future.

According to Investopedia, "The **1970s** saw some of the highest rates of **inflation** in the United States in recent history, with interest rates rising in turn to nearly 20%." (source: https://www.investopedia.com/articles/economics/09/1970s-great-inflation.asp).

Due to the tremendous amount of deficit spending in the United States in recent years, among other factors, several economists and other experts are predicting that inflation will rise significantly.

While inflation has been relatively low in recent years, almost all of us have noticed how much the price of cars, gasoline, food, cable television and other goods and services has soared.

Thirty years ago, a twenty-dollar bill would fill an entire grocery cart with food, and today, it barely covers the ingredients for one good meal. If you are having steak or salmon and a couple of side dishes, it may not pay for the ingredients of one meal.

Even a low rate of inflation compounded over the years can cut the spending value of your portfolio in half over time.

There are proven ways to keep up with inflation without taking unnecessary risks, and I am going to discuss those later in this book.

BUCKET #2:
Long term growth because of the silent killer of wealth called inflation

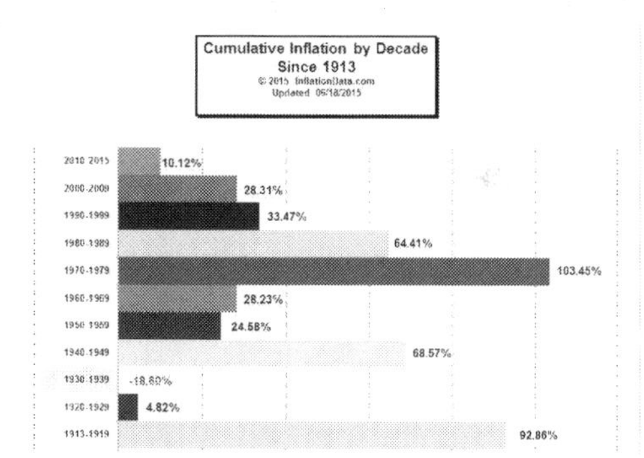

INFLATION:
THE PRACTICAL IMPACT

Your Third Bucket

Your third bucket is your **income bucket**. This bucket should provide you with reliable income that will last for the rest of your life. There are only three vehicles that guarantee income for life: Social Security, pensions and annuities.

It is important to note that some pension plans have become insolvent and are unable to pay the pensions that have been promised.

There are many misconceptions about annuities that need to be dealt with. I will be the first to admit that not all annuities are good. Some annuities are high-risk.

There are many different types of annuities and the key to success is to find an annuity from a strong insurance company that will help you reach your retirement income goals.

Social Security and pensions are in many ways similar to annuities. Ideally, each should provide you with an income stream during your retirement years.

Pensions and Social Security are relatively limited. One of the exciting benefits of annuities is that they are potentially almost unlimited.

Unlike a pension or Social Security, you can put as much money as you want into an annuity. The more money you put into an annuity, the higher your potential retirement income will be in retirement.

It would be best if you had this bucket to provide you income that will last as long as you live. If you are married, you need to make certain that you have enough money in your Income Bucket to last as long as either one of you might live. One of you might live to be over 100 years old and I hope you do.

With some annuities, when the owner dies, the remaining

principal in the annuity (if any) goes to the insurance company and the income stream stops. However, other annuities will continue to make income payments to a surviving spouse when one spouse passes away.

When I am advising couples, I almost always recommend the type of annuity that will provide a lifetime income stream to the surviving spouse when the first spouse passes away.

Some annuities are structured so that when both spouses pass away, their beneficiaries can receive the remaining balance in the annuity.

There are an almost endless variety of annuities today. There are annuities for every type of client and every purpose.

If you want an annuity that will pay you the **maximum guaranteed income** for 10 years and then cease payments, there is even an annuity that will help you reach that goal.

If you do not have a pension, rental property income or a large Social Security income, one of the best ways to make up for that income shortfall is to put as much money as you prudently can into a high-quality annuity.

This is one of the most powerful strategies you can use to create your own Personal Pension Plan.

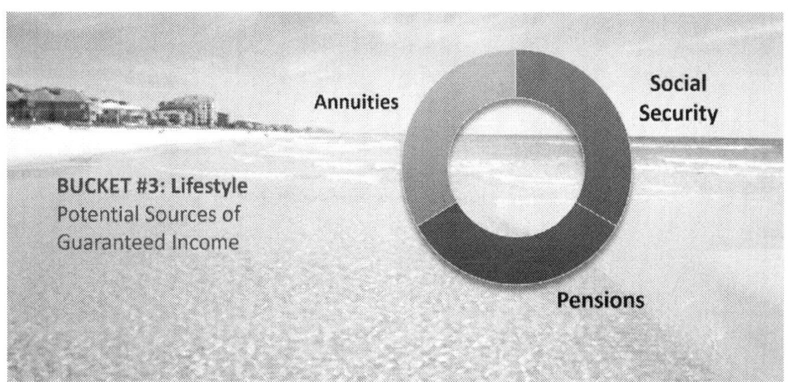

Your Fourth Bucket

Your fourth bucket is your Legacy Bucket. These are the funds and assets you want to leave for the next generation (your children, grandchildren, nieces and nephews and to charity).

A number of people feel guilty if they spend all their money and leave nothing for the next generation or charity. There is a **solution** that will enable you to leave substantial assets to the next generation—even if you think you can't afford right now to do much for them.

Special life insurance policies essentially enable you to buy dollar bills for a small fraction of the cost. This is accomplished via the tremendous leverage that only life insurance can provide.

There is also a way to leave these funds, which could be tens of thousands of dollars, hundreds of thousands of dollars, or MORE—to the next generation totally free of income taxes and estate taxes. This is accomplished through a very special type of trust.

The details of selecting the best life insurance policy and setting up one of these tax-free trusts can get a little complicated. That is why you will want to work with a trusted financial advisor who can make the process simple and enjoyable for you.

Once you have a great high-quality life insurance policy (and maybe also a life insurance trust—although this is NOT required), you will then be able to spend all of your money while you are still alive with no guilt. This is because, due to the insurance you own, you know that your spouse, your children and other loved ones and your favorite charities will all be financially taken care of.

Don't Live a "What if This Happens?" Life

I meet and work with many successful people every week.

I also meet people who have not planned well for their retirement and I have learned a lot from these people. What have I learned?

People who have not planned well for their retirement are constantly worried about money. The thoughts running through their minds are:

- **What if** I cannot pay my bills?
- **What if** I run out of money?
- **What happens if** inflation keeps going up and I can't maintain my lifestyle?
- **What if** the stock market crashes?
- **What if** I can't leave any money to my spouse and children?
- **What if** I can't pay for my medical expenses or long-term care?
- **You DON'T want to live a "What if this happens?" life full of worry.**

Related questions they ask themselves are:

- How can I ever live off this small Social Security check?
- How can I ever pay my bills with this microscopic amount of money I earn in bank interest?
- If you live a "What if" life full of financial worries, you cannot truly enjoy your retirement. You do NOT want to be one of those seniors constantly worried about "What if X, Y, or Z happens?"

I have dedicated my professional career to helping retirees and pre-retirees avoid having "what if…" worries.

My focus in retirement income planning and investment planning is on doing everything possible to help ensure that my clients can live a long, prosperous and happy retirement.

One of the ways I accomplish this is by helping my clients **avoid or remove roadblocks to retirement security** and that is what we will be focusing on in the next chapter.

CHAPTER THREE

ROADBLOCKS TO YOUR SUCCESSFUL, HAPPY AND PROSPEROUS RETIREMENT AND HOW TO OVERCOME THEM

Unfortunately, as we go through life, we inevitably encounter roadblocks.

Some roadblocks in life are relatively easy to overcome. However, planning for a happy and prosperous retirement is a complex task. Do not let this discourage you.

With proper guidance, you can overcome EVERY roadblock on your path to the retirement of your dreams.

In planning for retirement, you are likely to have to face and deal with four common roadblocks.

The First Roadblock to Retirement Success

This first roadblock is **longevity risk**. What does this term actually mean?

Longevity risk is a term used to describe the increasingly common situation in which people live longer or much longer than they had assumed and the **risk** is that they will run out of money in retirement.

We are living longer and healthier lives than any generation that came before us, so we have to make sure that we don't run out of money. With medical breakthroughs, better nutrition, organ transplants, etc., the human life span will likely increase.

Good retirement planning is not just about your immediate or **current living expenses** but also involves making sure you will have ALL the money you need to cover your **future living expenses** for as long as you may live.

The average life expectancy for a sixty-five-year-old man is about nineteen additional years (to age **84**). The average 65-year-old woman is expected to live another twenty-two years to age **87**.

Bear in mind that these are just averages and do not take into account individual circumstances. Fifty percent of people aged sixty-five will live longer than the above-stated life expectancy. Some of the readers of this book will live to be more than 100 years old. Do you have savings and investments to pay all of your expenses for all of those years of retirement?

None of us can predict how long we might live. No one has a crystal ball. For that reason, we must create a financial plan and have investments that will support us for even more years than the statistical tables say we might live.

One of the solutions that can help retirees deal with longevity risk is annuities. Annuities can be very complex because there are many annuities ranging from short-term fixed annuities to deferred long term annuities. Some annuities pay a simple guaranteed interest rate and there are annuities whose return is linked to a stock market index. There are also variable annuities that I generally do not recommend.

Due to the complexity of annuities, you want to work with a financial advisor or insurance expert who is very knowledgeable about this product class. Other assets that can help deal with longevity risk are pensions, IRAs and 401(K)'s.

Working with a caring and knowledgeable financial advisor who can integrate all of these assets, along with mutual funds, real estate, cash and other assets, into a sophisticated financial plan that can help you successfully deal with longevity risk. This is one of the best ways of ensuring that you will have all the money you need to support your retirement lifestyle as long as you may live.

The Second Roadblock to a Successful Retirement

This second roadblock is **inflation risk**; as time goes by, the value of money becomes less and less. We have all noticed that a dollar today buys much LESS than it did 10 years ago or 20 years ago.

Ten years from now, a dollar will buy much less than it does today due to the wealth-eroding effects of inflation.

To deal with the inflation risk roadblock, you will need investments that keep up with inflation and perhaps even exceed inflation. Investments like stocks, bonds, real estate, and tax-deferred annuities are examples of vehicles you can use to keep up with inflation.

Inflation is the silent thief that steals from all of us. Every year, most of the essentials of life become more expensive. While a few may become less expensive, others will skyrocket so high in price that it drives up the overall cost of living.

The **CPI** is the measure of the weighted average of prices in a basket of consumer goods and services which are typical purchases for households. These goods and services include transportation, food and medical care items. The Index is calculated by taking price changes for each item in the predetermined basket of goods and averaging them. The CPI is used as a measure of the annual percentage of inflation.

Many experts believe the CPI understates real inflation because there are many things we need to purchase that are either not included in the CPI or "adjusted" using various formulas.

Also, it is essential not just to keep up with inflation but also to have investments that can significantly exceed the inflation rate and thus offer a higher degree of protection. For example, a Fixed-Indexed Annuity tied to the gains of the stock market while protecting you when the market goes down may be a great solution. There are various names for these annuities and they are sometimes referred to as "Equity-Indexed Annuities" or "Equity-Linked Annuities."

Some of these Equity-Indexed Annuities (EIAs) are uncapped, meaning you can get much higher returns when the stock market has a good year. However, unlike a mutual fund, with an EIA, you will not lose money if the stock market goes down.

This book is being written in 2021. The stock market has been going up since 2009 with only a few relatively brief breaks (one brought on by coronavirus). This is a very long and very old bull market.

We all know nothing goes up forever, including the stock market. With a Bull Market that is this old, it's not a question **if** but **when** the market will go down—and how severe the pull-back will be.

We have had crashes where the stock market lost approximately 40% of its value in one year. **Could you afford to lose 40% of the value of your life savings that is in stocks?**

You do not have to worry about that when you own certain high-quality annuities or other protected assets.

Doesn't it make sense to protect what you have worked so hard to accumulate while still getting good returns when the market goes up? That is what a carefully selected fixed-indexed annuity could offer you.

The truth is you don't need to take high risks to get good and often great returns on your money.

The Third Roadblock to Your Retirement Success

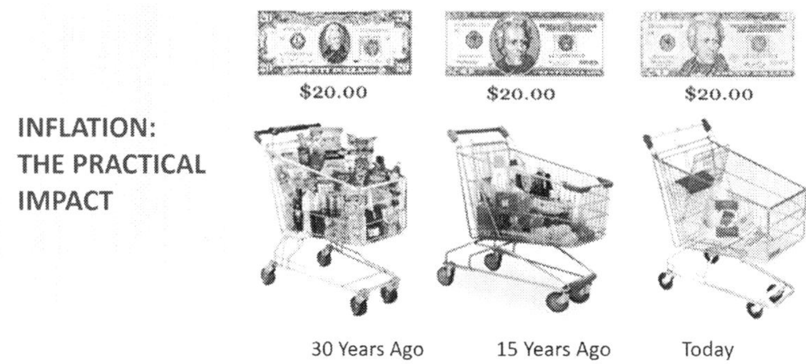

This third roadblock to your retirement success is **disability**: The possibility that you might become disabled, become unable to work, may need long-term care. More people become disabled each year than die. Unfortunately, most people greatly underestimate the odds that they will become disabled and when disability happens, they are totally unprepared for it.

This is a topic I hold dear to my heart. Over the years I have seen clients struggle both financially and emotionally dealing with taking care of a loved one. Not only that but I have experienced this first hand with my Mom. About Seven years ago my Mom was diagnosed with Alzheimer's. Fortunately, my brother lived very close by so he and his family could take turns providing care for Mom. Eventually mom needed 24 hour care which my brother could not provide, so we had to hire outside help. Her care cost was over $10,000 a month for about four years, fortunately we had policies and funds set aside for her care. This could have been a huge burden on the family had we not planned for her care in advance.

The question I often get is "What is Long Term Care?" Long Term Care is not being able to do two of the six daily living activities such as:

Transferring (Getting out of Bed)
Bathing
Dressing
Toileting
Eating
Continence

Typically, when you need help with two of these six activities of daily living, you need long-term care.

Or, if you have a cognitive impairment like Alzheimer's Disease or Dementia you may need long term care.

Most people think that Long Term Care takes place in a nursing home, but in fact 80% of the care takes place at home.

Did you know that 70% of the people over 65 will need long term care during their lifetime?

Did also know that 700,000 people suffer from stroke every year? That is every 40 seconds someone has a stroke in America. One in ten people age 65 or older have Alzheimer's and 33% of people age 85 or older have Alzheimer's. In the US over 53 Million people have osteoporosis.

The solution for dealing with this retirement roadblock is a carefully selected **long-term care (LTC) policy.** Unfortunately, the cost of long-term care keeps soaring, and you can't afford to use up all your life savings to pay for just a few years of long-term care expenses.

If you do not own a high-quality long-term care policy, you could quickly wipe out your retirement savings. Unfortunately, several retirees (or their children) have been forced to sell the family home to pay for long-term care or nursing home care expenses. **In some parts of the country, the costs of long-term care can exceed $100,000 per year.**

What many people do not realize is that unless you are desperately poor, you will not qualify for government assistance in paying for long-term care.

I ask my clients, "If you needed long-term care, where would you like to receive it?" Almost everyone answers, "In my home."

I very rarely hear someone say, "I want to go to a nursing home."

Also, most people do not want to become a burden to their children or be forced to live in a tiny back bedroom or down in the basement of the home of an adult child.

With proper planning, most seniors and retirees CAN stay in their own homes for their entire lives or nearly their whole lives. As long as the living situation is safe and comfortable, seniors can continue to live at home and have high-quality home health care provided by highly trained professionals. All of this can be paid for by a long-term care insurance policy.

More than 45% of those age 65 to 74 and 70% of people 75 or older reported difficulty in some activity of daily living and need long term care assistance. Some people need help getting dressed, others need help bathing, others need help with mobility (walking or moving about in a wheelchair). Others need help preparing meals or eating.

Today, there are insurance policies that will pay your Long Term Care expenses **on a tax free basis**.

What if you never need long term care and you have been paying on that policy for many years? There are some breakthrough new policies that say **if you never need to use the LTC benefits, we will give you back ALL of your money at the end of the term of the policy if you meet certain requirements**.

There are also policies that will give you extra benefits without your having to qualify.

This issue of paying for Long Term Care has become a huge burden to the Government. As a result the Government has also introduced back in 2010 The Pension Protection Act which provides tax incentives to help pay for long term care. As you can see, Long-Term Care policies provide many choices and many options.

Let me give you some examples of what we did with our clients.

John age 70 had $300,000 in savings, $35,000 in his checking account and he bought an annuity a few years ago for $100,000

that was now worth $200,000. He was recently widowed and his adult children lived out of town. He cares deeply about remaining in his home if he needed care. He also had some health issues—controlled diabetes with history of heart disease and was turned down by traditional long term care insurance. I asked John, "If you needed care which assets would use to pay for your care? He said, "I would cash in my Annuity." I said, "If you did that you would pay taxes on the $100,000 growth in the annuity." I then asked him, "If there was a better way, would you want to know about it?" He said, "Absolutely."

We did, we took his $200,000 annuity converted it into a Pension Protection Act Annuity which immediately gave him a bucket worth $500,000 to pay for long Term Care Tax Free. So if he needed Care, he would receive $8,300 a month Tax Free to pay for Home Care, Assisted Living and skilled care. Remember the $100,000 growth in the annuity that was taxable, now became all tax free. Not only that his bucket to pay for Long Term Care grew two and a half times from $200,000 to $500,000 to pay for Care.

Let me give another example.

Joan, age 63, has a history of Alzheimer's Disease in her family which has her very concerned. She has $250,000 in an IRA, $370,000 in CD's and $300,000 in Stocks and Bonds. I asked, "If you became ill which asset would you use to pay for your Care?" She said, "Probably my CD's." I said, "If there was a better way would you want to know about it? She said, "Absolutely." We took $150,000 out of her CD's and gave her a bucket worth $525,391 tax free to pay for Long Term Care, which would pay her $7,297 a month tax free for Home Health Care, Assisted

Living and Skilled Care. She also has a cash indemnity which means she can pay a friend or relative with these funds to help take care of her. If she never needs care and ten years went by, she can get all her money refunded to her.

How about one more example? Tim (age 63) and Patty (age 61).

They have $700,000 in an IRA, $37,000 on Checking and $250,000 in CD's.

Patty is frightened by the idea of going into a nursing home.

Tim and Patty are not big fans of Traditional Long Term Care, the one where you pay monthly premiums which could go up and if you don't use it use lose it.

Tim and Patty also want to leave a legacy to their kids.I asked the same question "If you needed care which asset would you use First?" They said Tim's IRA. I then said if there was a better way would they want to know about it? They both said absolutely.

We took $200,000, a portion of their IRA, and immediately created an unlimited bucket to pay for Long Term Care. This would pay $6,685 a month for Tim's or Patty's Care or both for up to $13,370 a month tax free to pay for their care. If they both passed away and never needed the care their beneficiaries would receive $221,841 tax free. This converted taxable IRA money to tax free money and unlimited benefits to pay for care.

We have several more cases where we helped clients who had Parkinson's or veterans that had additional benefits to pay for their care.

As you can see, Long-Term Care policies provide many choices and many options. To figure out which policy is best for you and/or your spouse, you should speak with a financial advisor who has deep expertise in the area of LTC policies.

The Fourth Roadblock To Your Retirement Success

What if the stock market goes down? What if it goes down significantly? This happened in 2001 during the dot-com bubble crash, and it happened again in 2008 during the Great Recession when many stocks fell by 50% to 60% or even more. Even index funds took huge losses during these market crashes.

If you are young and the stock market crashes, you may have time to re-build your portfolio and your net worth. However, **what happens if the stock market crashes in the five years prior to your retirement?** Will you have time to rebuild your retirement nest egg?

The five years before you retire is known as the "retirement danger zone" or the "retirement red zone." This red zone also extends to the five years AFTER you retire, so **it covers a 10-year period of time where extra caution with your investments is warranted**. (See Chart 3.1)

If you have a bad investment experience in the stock market or real estate market during that period, you could put all of your retirement dreams at risk.

The specific type of risk we are referring to here is called **Sequence of Returns Risk**.

The definition of Sequence of Return Risk is "the risk that market declines in the early years of retirement, paired with ongoing withdrawals, could significantly reduce the longevity of a portfolio." (Source: https://www.forbes.com/advisor/retirement/sequence-of-returns-risk/).

Suppose you experience a stock market or real estate market crash early in retirement and begin withdrawing money for retirement income from assets that are down in value (effectively locking in losses every month that we take money out for income). In that case, we can create a downward spiral on our retirement accounts from which it is almost impossible to recover.

The net result is that you could run out of money much sooner than you ever anticipated.

Chart 3.1

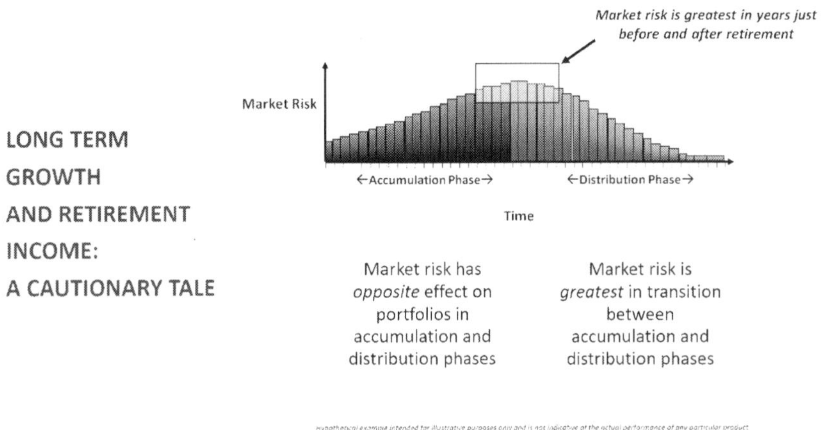

Here is a hypothetical example of what sequence of return risk can look like.(see chart 3.2)

Let's look at two retirees, Mr. Smith and Ms. Jones. They each start off their retirements with $100,000 in investments with 60% in stocks and 40% in bonds. They each begin withdrawing $5,000 a year in income and they both live 30 years in retirement.

Notably, Mr. Smith ended up with a superior rate of return (10.5% to Ms. Jones 9.6%) and yet he ended up running out of money 10 years before he died. However, **Ms. Jones never ran out of money and indeed saw her nest egg grow to $591,402 at the time of her death**. The difference is the year each person began their retirement.

Mr. Smith began his retirement in **1969**, right before a bear market began, and Ms. Jones began her retirement in **1979**, right before a major bull market started. **The dramatic difference in how their retirements turned out was due to the sequence of investment returns they each experienced.**

The challenge we each face is that none of us has a crystal ball to predict how the stock market will behave over the next 20 to 30 years of our retirement. The obvious problem is we can't know in advance what those critical early years of retirement will look like in the financial markets.

The key is to position our assets in such a manner that our income is not dependent on the vagaries of the market. Therefore, it behooves us to look for solutions that will provide **safe and reliable income in retirement.**

Here are just a few of the pros and cons of various **ways of generating retirement income**:

1.) Stock Dividends

Pros: Possible market upside for the stocks and decent, although not great, income from dividends.
Cons: Stocks can go down and sometimes crash. Stock dividends are not guaranteed and a company can stop paying dividends.

2.) Bond Interest

Pros: Steady income that is potentially higher than stock dividends. Bond interest is less volatile than stock dividends. In

Chart 3.2

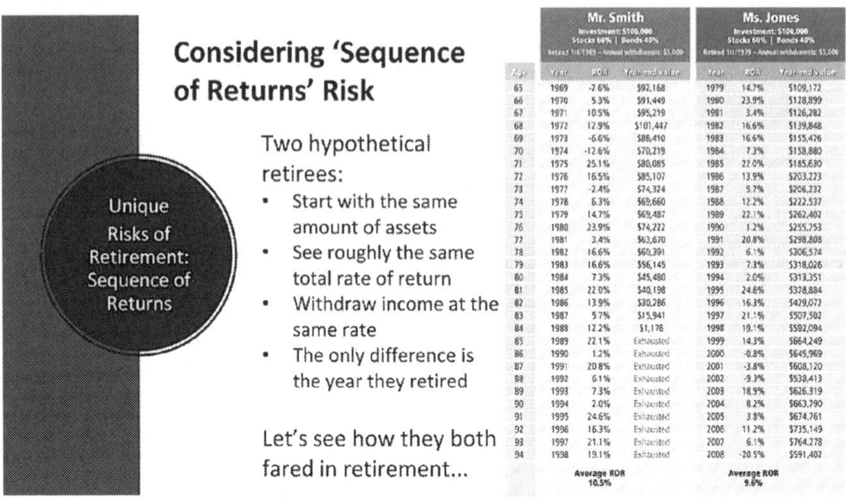

	Mr. Smith Investment: $100,000 Stocks 60% | Bonds 40% Retired 1/1/1969 – Annual withdrawals: $5,000			Ms. Jones Investment: $100,000 Stocks 60% | Bonds 40% Retired 1/1/1979 – Annual withdrawals: $5,000		
Age	Year	ROR	Year-end value	Year	ROR	Year-end value
65	1969	-7.6%	$92,168	1979	14.7%	$109,172
66	1970	5.3%	$91,449	1980	23.9%	$128,899
67	1971	10.5%	$95,219	1981	3.4%	$126,282
68	1972	12.9%	$101,447	1982	16.6%	$139,848
69	1973	-6.6%	$88,410	1983	16.6%	$155,426
70	1974	-12.6%	$70,219	1984	7.3%	$158,880
71	1975	25.1%	$80,085	1985	22.0%	$185,630
72	1976	16.5%	$85,107	1986	13.9%	$203,223
73	1977	-2.4%	$74,324	1987	5.7%	$206,232
74	1978	6.3%	$69,660	1988	12.2%	$222,537
75	1979	14.7%	$69,487	1989	22.1%	$262,402
76	1980	23.9%	$74,222	1990	1.2%	$255,753
77	1981	3.4%	$63,670	1991	20.8%	$298,808
78	1982	16.6%	$60,391	1992	6.1%	$306,574
79	1983	16.6%	$56,145	1993	7.3%	$318,026
80	1984	7.3%	$45,480	1994	2.0%	$313,351
81	1985	22.0%	$40,198	1995	24.6%	$378,884
82	1986	13.9%	$30,286	1996	16.3%	$429,072
83	1987	5.7%	$15,941	1997	21.1%	$507,502
84	1988	12.2%	$1,176	1998	19.1%	$592,094
85	1989	22.1%	Exhausted	1999	14.3%	$664,249
86	1990	1.2%	Exhausted	2000	-0.8%	$645,969
87	1991	20.8%	Exhausted	2001	-3.8%	$608,120
88	1992	6.1%	Exhausted	2002	-9.3%	$538,413
89	1993	7.3%	Exhausted	2003	18.9%	$626,319
90	1994	2.0%	Exhausted	2004	8.2%	$663,790
91	1995	24.6%	Exhausted	2005	3.8%	$674,761
92	1996	16.3%	Exhausted	2006	11.2%	$735,149
93	1997	21.1%	Exhausted	2007	6.1%	$764,278
94	1998	19.1%	Exhausted	2008	-20.5%	$591,402
		Average ROR 10.5%			Average ROR 9.6%	

addition, some bonds are guaranteed by the issuer and some bonds are insured.

Cons: Bond interest rates are very low now compared to historical standards. Companies or municipalities can get into financial trouble, suspend dividends, or stop paying them entirely if they go out of business.

3.) Social Security

Pros: Income is guaranteed for life and backed up by the U.S. government.

Cons: Your monthly payment from Social Security probably won't cover all your income needs and if one spouse passes away, you lose the lower Social Security benefit. Also, experts believe that Social Security is underfunded and believe there is a fairly high probability that Social Security benefits may have to be reduced in future years (source: https://www.marketwatch.com/story/the-financial-hole-for-social-security-and-medicare-is-even-deeper-than-the-experts-say-2018-06-15).

4.) Fixed indexed annuities

Pros: Provides a contractually guaranteed lifetime income stream without stock market risk.
Cons: These are long-term investments and many have surrender charges if cashed in early. The surrender charges do not apply if taking an income stream and if you hold them for the required amount of time.

Also, the guarantee is provided by the issuing insurance company. If the insurance company gets into financial trouble, the income may not be delivered. However, this is so rare it is almost non-existent.

Here is a chart showing how an indexed annuity performed from 1999 to the present versus the S & P 500.

The Grey Line reflects the **S & P 500** and the Purple Line represents a **fixed indexed annuity**. As you can see, every year on its anniversary date, the Annuity locks in its gains from the previous year and you never lose them if the market goes down.

A Fixed Indexed Annuity offers **principal protection** and will never lose value due to a stock market decline. For example, **if you put $500,000 into a fixed indexed annuity, it will NEVER be worth less than $500,000 even if the stock market loses 40% of its value.**

Chart 3.3

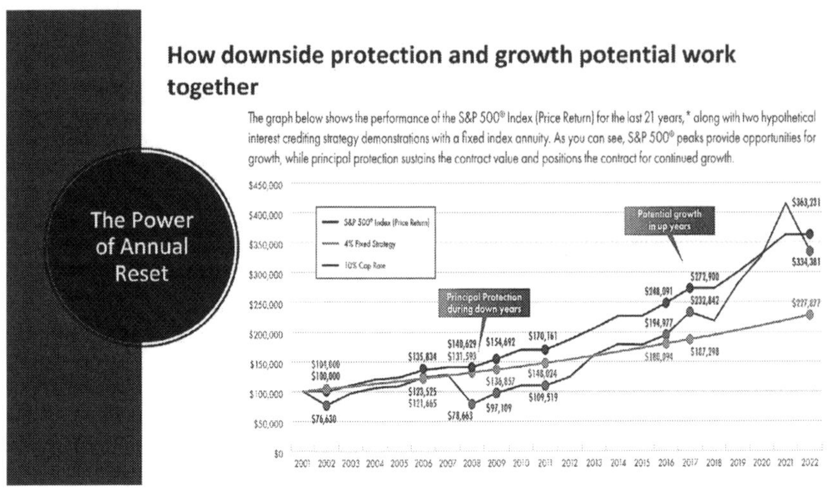

Indexed annuities are contractually guaranteed by the claims-paying ability of the issuing insurance company. You are essentially passing on your market risk from yourself to a major US Corporation. It is important to work with an annuity expert to make certain you are buying a fixed index annuity from a financially strong insurance company.

The next chart will show how long it to recover from previous bear markets.

Chart 3.4

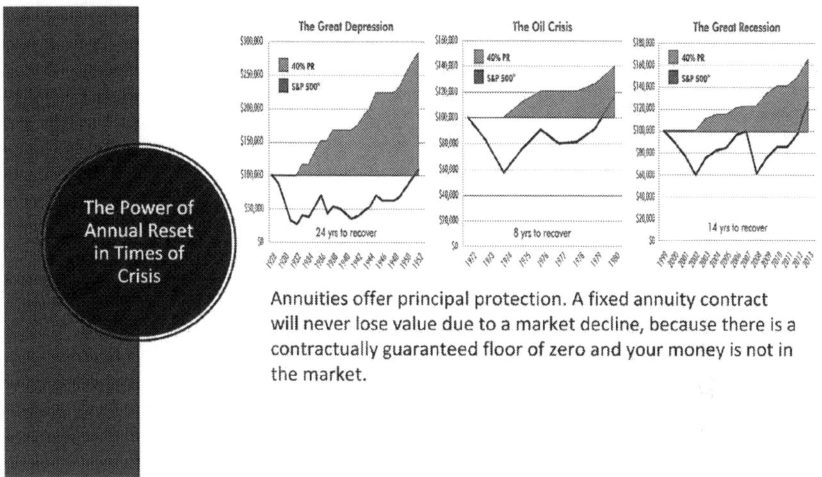

Annuities offer principal protection. A fixed annuity contract will never lose value due to a market decline, because there is a contractually guaranteed floor of zero and your money is not in the market.

What is the Biggest Roadblock of them all?

I believe that the biggest roadblock, hands down, is **longevity risk**. Why do I say that? The longer you live, the greater the chance that you will run out of money.

Unless you are rich, each year, you will have to spend more of your retirement nest egg—so it will shrink.

Due to inflation, the remaining dollars in your retirement nest egg will be worth less and will buy less.

Also, the longer you live, the greater the chance that you will run into a stock market debacle like those that happened in 2001 and 2008.

The longer you live, the greater the chance that you may become disabled and need long-term care or nursing home care, which is very expensive.

What if we could take longevity risk off the table? I believe we can.

According to some experts, stocks, bonds, real estate, CDs, and money markets accounts cannot take longevity risk off the table—only annuities can. An article published by the Boston College, National Risk Index study, states: "Ensuring retirement security for an aging population is one of the most compelling challenges facing the nation. The main focus is ensuring that retirees have a large enough nest egg. However, to achieve real security in retirement, households need to get out of their nest egg as much as possible during the drawdown period. Annuities guarantee that households do not outlive their money. Finally, **annuities provide more monthly income than any other approaches**, such as the 4 percent rule or living off the interest of your assets." (Boston College, National Risk Index Study, October 2010.)

Chart 3.5

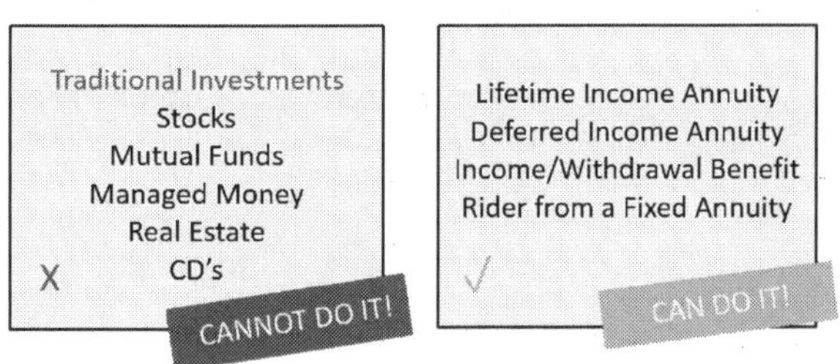

"Ensuring retirement security for an aging population is one of the most compelling challenges facing the nation. The main focus these days is ensuring that retirees have a large enough nest egg. However, to achieve real security in retirement, households need to get as much as possible out of their nest eggs during the drawdown period. Annuities guarantee that households do not outlive their money. Finally, annuities provide more monthly income than other approaches, such as the 4 percent Rule or living off the interest of assets."

-- Boston College, National Risk Index Study, October 2010

Remember the previously cited example (Chart 3.2) of Mr. Smith, who had to move in with his children. Mr. Smith ran out of money and could not financially support himself for the last 10 years of his retirement. If he had invested his funds in a carefully selected annuity, he could have received what are called **longevity credits**.

With longevity credits, even if Mr. Smith's account went to zero, **he would continue to get his monthly income check from the annuity for as long as he lived**.

In the chart below (3.6), the **Dark** bars represent his investment and the **blue bars** show his interest earned **and the yellow line is longevity credits**.

You are probably asking yourself, **"How can insurance companies do that?"** Insurance companies have actuaries that mathematically calculate these risks. In addition, they maintain huge reserves (hundreds of millions of dollars or more) and **they carefully select and purchase conservative investments that enable them to pay you income for life—regardless of how long you live**.

In this way, insurance companies are uniquely able to eliminate longevity risk.

Chart 3.6

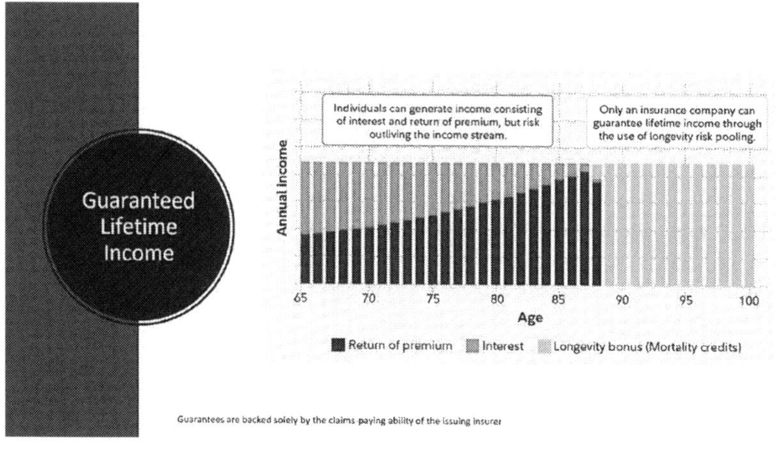

the risks of living too long and outliving your money.

In addition, insurance companies are able to protect your family and loved ones from the risk that you may die too young. When you buy an insurance policy, you do not have to worry about the risk of dying too young. If you are called to Heaven early, the insurance company can provide your family with hundreds of thousands to millions of dollars to live on, depending on the size of the insurance policy you purchased.

Be sure to speak with an insurance expert to find the types of annuities and insurance policies that best fit your financial needs and your budget.

CHAPTER FOUR

STOCKBROKER VS. MY POWERFUL FOUR-BUCKET SYSTEM

Most stockbrokers only use **one bucket**, which is their stock, mutual fund, ETF, bond and cash portfolio.

This seems like a lot, but upon reflection, you will note that none of these investments is truly protected except the cash component—and that is not protected against inflation.

Bonds or bond funds can be protected by buying insurance, but this adds an extra cost and reduces the yield.

When you want less risk, a broker will typically reduce the percentage of your assets in stocks, mutual funds, and ETFs and increase your investments in bonds or bond funds. As you are probably aware, **bonds and bond funds, just like stocks, can decline in value.** Historically, bonds are less volatile than stocks, but if interest rates go up (as many experts are now predicting they will), bond values will decline.

We have been in one of the lowest interest-rate environments in decades. When interest rates are this low, often the only direction they can move is UP and sometimes interest rates move dramatically upward as they did in 1980 and 1981.

Rising interest rates will drive up the cost of borrowing money, **they will drive up the cost for business everywhere** and businesses will pass those costs on to consumers. We are already seeing this take place.

As I am writing this book in 2021, gasoline and food prices are at multi-year highs. Commodity prices are hitting multi-year highs. Used cars are at or near all-time record highs. Pharmaceutical drugs and college tuition are at or near all-time highs. Many of the necessities of life are at or near all-time highs in price. In many cities and towns, the cost to rent a home is at or near an all-time high.

Many experts believe prices are going to continue to rise. THE TIME TO PROTECT YOURSELF IS NOW—before prices rise any further.

How Does the One Bucket System Work?

When you need money for emergencies or to pay expenses, your broker will sell some of the stocks, mutual funds, ETFs, or bonds in your portfolio and will provide you with the cash. However, what happens if the market is down when your broker sells these investments?

If you sell into a declining market, you may be locking in losses from which you cannot recover.

If you continue selling into a declining market, you could run out of money much sooner—years sooner—than you ever thought possible.

This is exactly what happened to some retirees in 2000 to 2002 and 2008 and 2009. They ran out of money, or their reserves got so low they were forced to go back to work just to get by.

You do not want to suffer the same fate. To avoid such outcome, it is wise to move some of your investment funds into protected investments that will NOT decline in value no matter how far the stock market falls. You also want these investments to produce the **reliable income** you will need.

A retirement income specialist can help you make smart investment choices that will help you accomplish the above goals.

The Significance of the 4% Rule

The Four Percent Rule is a rough guide to figure out how much money a retired person should withdraw from their retirement portfolio each year.

The Four Percent Rule is based on stock and bond returns studies over a 50-year period spanning from **1926 to 1976**.

The goal of the Four Percent Rule is to try to determine how much money can be safely taken out of investments and savings each year to provide an income stream to retirees. The risk is in taking out too much money—which could rapidly deplete your retirement nest egg.

You want your retirement nest egg to last as long as you do—or even longer if you wish to leave something for your spouse or loved ones.

The Four Percent Rule is used to determine what is called the portfolio withdrawal rate. According to this Rule, on a **$100,000 portfolio, you could safely withdraw and spend $4,000 a year**. On a **$1 million portfolio, you could safely withdraw and spend $40,000 a year.**

For many years, brokers used the 4% Rule to withdraw funds from your investment portfolio. However, as you have just read, if the stock market incurs significant losses in the early years of your retirement, if you withdraw 4% of your money every year from this shrunken portfolio, you could rapidly run out of money.

Many experts believe the 4% Rule is not prudent or safe and they recommend a 2%-3% withdrawal rate. However, even using a 2% withdrawal rate in a declining stock market does NOT guarantee that you will not run out of money.

Brokers and others who use the 4% Rule sometimes use what are knowns as "**Monte Carlo simulations**" to try to provide a probability of how long your money might last in retirement. According to **Investopedia**, "Monte Carlo simulations are used to model the probability of different outcomes in a process that cannot easily be predicted due to the intervention of random variables. It is a technique used to understand the impact of risk and uncertainty in prediction and forecasting models."(source: **https://www.investopedia.com/terms/m/montecarlosimulation.asp**)

Notice all of the qualifier words in that definition: "probability," "in a process that cannot easily be predicted," "random variables," "risk," and "uncertainty."

These are NOT words or terms that provide peace of mind. If you want certainty and guarantees, the 4% Rule and Monte Carlo simulations probably cannot offer what you want.

High-quality income annuities and fixed annuities do provide solid guarantees and can provide steady retirement income for as long as you live. If guarantees are of interest to you, a wise investment of your time would be to book a meeting with an annuity expert.

The stock market required more than 20 years to recover from the losses it suffered during the Great Depression. The stock market took eight years to recover from the "oil shock" of the early 1970s.

The Great Recession, which started around 2008, inflicted so much damage on the stock market that it took 14 years just to break even, not counting the time value of money or lost opportunity.

Remember that while the stock market is recovering, your money is losing value every year due to inflation. Therefore, if you had $100,000 worth of stock before a stock market crash and after 10 years, your stocks recovered back to $100,000 in value, you actually lost spending power. Why is that?

Due to the wealth-eroding effects of inflation, today's $100,000 does not buy what $100,000 could purchase 10 years ago. If inflation is only 2% per year, after 10 years, your $100,000 has lost about 20% of its spending power. In other words, your $100,000 only has about $80,000 in spending power left.

What would happen if you take income from your portfolio while the stock market is declining?

This is like a double-whammy to your retirement nest egg. The stock market itself is shrinking your portfolio and the money you are taking from your investment portfolio is the second whammy. This is how retirement nest eggs can get wiped out in only a few years. Obviously, the best time to protect your retirement nest egg is NOW, before the next stock market crash occurs.

When you take money out of a declining stock market portfolio, you are locking in losses each time you sell a stock, mutual fund, or ETF. This can lead to what is called a portfolio death spiral.

Why is it called a death spiral? It is because it is a series of losses you might never be able to recover from and that could lead to financial ruin. I have dedicated my entire professional career to trying to protect people from such losses.

It is OK to speculate in the stock market when you are younger. However, when you are approaching or at retirement age, it makes much more sense to become more conservative with your money.

Do you want to base your retirement security on the vagaries and whims of the stock market?

If not, you should take comfort in knowing that you CAN enjoy significant growth in your portfolio without subjecting yourself to major stock market risk.

One of the methods I have found most successful in accomplishing this is using my **Four Bucket System**.

You can have a bucket containing investments that generate a steady safe income. And, you can have a bucket that contains high-quality growth investments that will protect you from inflation for years or even decades to come. You can even have a bucket that contains legacy investments that will give you the power to leave money and assets to your spouse, children, loved ones and favorite charities.

From 1973 to 1995, a portfolio of 50% stocks and 50% bonds achieved an average annual return of 10.1%. This is a very good rate of return for a reasonably conservative portfolio. If you held on to your stocks and bonds during this time period, you would have been fine.

But what would have happened if you retired in 1973 and start taking income out of your portfolio at the rate of 5% per year?

You might think that you would be fine since that time

period showed an average annual return of 10.1%. Unfortunately, in 1973 and 1974, the stock market went down while you were taking your 5% income. Therefore, it was like digging a hole in your portfolio with two shovels.

One shovel was the stock market itself taking value out of your retirement nest egg and the second shovel was your own personal withdrawals to pay your bills.

This example highlights why using a "one-bucket system" to manage your retirement nest egg is so dangerous.

No one has a crystal ball. No one can predict what the stock market will do today, tomorrow, or the day after that. Nobody knows when the market will go down or go up.

Don't base your retirement security on making guesses about the stock market. As you have learned in this chapter and previous chapters, **you CAN enjoy retirement security and have financial peace of mind.**

In upcoming chapters, we will delve into more detail on how you can enjoy financial security during retirement. **With the right kind of financial planning and the proper mix of investments, insurance, annuities and savings, millions of Americans are now enjoying total financial security in retirement**.

You now have an **opportunity** to join them.

CHAPTER FIVE

THE RETURN ON YOUR INVESTMENT

What is ROI? To some, it is "return on investment," but to me, it is "**reliability of income**." I truly enjoy helping my clients create a **reliable stream of passive income in retirement** so that they will have all the money they need without having to work.

Return on investment is a performance measure that can be used to compare several investments. ROI is calculated as the net income of an investment divided by the cost of the investment.

ROI = Net income / Investment cost

Net Income = Income from the investment minus investment cost.

For example, if **net income** is **$1,200** and investment cost is $10,000, then the **ROI** is 1,200/10,000 = 0.12 or stated as a percentage, **the ROI is 12%.**

An investment with an ROI of 12% could be an outstanding investment, but **only if the risk and volatility are relatively low.** As you approach or enter retirement, you generally want to minimize your exposure to high-risk and high-volatility investments.

If the ROI is negative, it means you are losing money on an investment. For example, if you bought a rental house and the rent you collect is not enough to pay for the mortgage, insurance, repairs and other costs, the rental house would have a negative rate of return.

As you approach or enter retirement, you want to try to avoid investments with a negative ROI. However, your entire focus should be on enjoying gains and minimizing or avoiding losses on your investments.

Generally speaking, a higher ROI is better than a lower ROI—but only if you can keep both risk and volatility low.

When you're young, you can take more risks because if an investment goes bad, you have many years (or even decades) to recover from that loss.

When you are older, you don't have much time to recover from investment losses. Therefore, most people in their mid-fifties and older should seek out low-risk investments that will produce reliable income that will last for the rest of their lives.

The success of your retirement is not about the size of your assets. **As long as you have enough money to pay all of your expenses and live the lifestyle you want in retirement, you are a success**.

Risks to Retirement Assets

There are many risks to your assets and you should do everything you can to protect them. For example, assets can be **lost** (you can lose a diamond ring, or a rare stamp, or a rare baseball card). In addition, assets can be **stolen** (Someone might steal the gold coins you hid in your bedroom).

It is estimated that more than 40 million lawsuits are filed in the United States every year (source: https://www.onelegal.com/blog/top-court-filing-statistics-from-around-the-country/). A number of retirees have lost some or all of their assets because they lost a lawsuit and were served with a judgment.

Another major risk to your assets is **divorce**. In many states, you could lose half of your assets in a divorce and the family home might also have to be sold. That one home might then have to be replaced by two homes or apartments, one for the ex-husband and one for the ex-wife, significantly driving up living costs for each person. Hopefully, you will not have to go through a divorce in retirement.

Your assets and net worth can be decimated in a **stock market crash** or **real estate crash**. Both of these occurred in the Great Recession around 2008 and 2009 and millions of Americans lost their homes to foreclosure.

Reliable income is at the heart of a successful retirement. Securing a basic level of lifetime income should be one of the top priorities of every retiree if they want to enjoy a happy and low-stress retirement.

How to Insure Against Risks

As you have learned in the above section (and from your own life experiences), there are many risks to investment.

Insurance is the ONE product specifically designed to help protect a person from risk or help a person (or a family) recover from a setback or a tragedy. The two insurance products we will look at here are **life insurance** and **annuities**. When you are young or middle-aged, you buy life insurance in case you die too soon. Life insurance guarantees that your family or loved ones will receive a certain sum of money (for example, $500,000 or $1 million or more) if you are called to heaven too early.

If you are in reasonably good health, today you can even buy life insurance if you are in your **60s** or **70s**—or, in some cases, even into your 80s.

You do NOT have to be in perfect health to buy life insurance. There are policies that are called "**simplified issue**" that only require you to answer about four simple questions. I have helped many of my clients obtain high-quality life insurance with these policies.

Some companies will even provide life insurance to people who take a variety of medications or who have recovered from cancer, a heart attack, or a stroke.

In other cases, if your health is relatively good, you can **get high-quality life insurance without having to take a physical or give a blood sample**. I have helped many of my clients obtain life insurance without having to go through these embarrassing or painful procedures.

The second insurance product you should seriously consider is **Annuities**. When you are older, you want to own annuities in case you live too long. **Annuities are one of the only financial products that can guarantee a reliable lifetime income that you cannot out-live**—even if you live to be 130.

In the previous chapter, I wrote about the risks of using a **One Bucket system**. One of the most significant risks is that if the stock market declines during a time period when you need to take money out of your portfolio, due to the combination of the stock market losses and your withdrawals, you risk having your retirement nest egg devastated—or—even running out of money.

If your money was in the proper type of annuity, you would not suffer from a stock market decline or even a stock market crash. Some annuities have returns that are linked to the stock market but your money is not directly invested in the stock market.

Other annuities offer guaranteed returns (income) that are entirely unrelated to the stock market. The insurance company guarantees that you will receive a monthly income stream for the rest of your life. If you have selected a **Joint Life Annuity, the income stream will continue as long as you or your spouse lives**.

With an annuity, you transfer the risk of living too long and running out of money from yourself to a large US corporation with hundreds of millions of dollars or billions of dollars to back up its claims-paying ability.

You have insurance to help deal with almost every risk in your life. Doesn't it make sense to protect your retirement account against stock market risk? You insure your home if it burns down, you insure your car in case of an accident or replace it if it is stolen, and you have health insurance to help pay for health care. Many people also have insurance for appliances or cell phones.

Doesn't it make sense to insure against one of the biggest risks

of all—that you might run out of money in retirement? That is the type of insurance—and **peace of mind**—that an annuity and only an annuity can provide.

As you have learned in this chapter, you need to **transition your thinking from return on investment to reliability of income.** For people over the age of fifty, it's not so much about becoming rich but making darn sure you don't get poor.

Time magazine featured an article about lifetime income stream as the key to happiness. It said:

"Securing at least the base level of income should be every retiree's priority at least if they want to live happily ever after." (Source: https://business.time.com/2012/07/30/lifetime-income-stream-key-to-retirement-happiness/)

Reliable income is at the heart of every successful retirement plan. The practical goal is that you do not want to run out of money before you die. The **personal pay-off** is that you will be able to enjoy every day of your retirement knowing that you have all the money you need to pay all of your bills, travel and live the lifestyle you desire.

While many retirees and pre-retirees are concerned about return ON investments, what deserves just as much attention is the return OF your investments. For that reason, you need to have SAFE investments that are guaranteed to produce reliable income year after year as long as you live.

Remember the lessons of the Great Recession of 2008 and 2009 (which lasted much longer than that in some parts of the country). Some people got so wrapped up in chasing high returns that they invested in real estate with too much-borrowed money, or they had too much of their life savings invested in the stock market right before it crashed. As you know, a number of retirees had to go back to work just to earn enough money to pay their basic living expenses.

I never want my clients to be in a position of being forced to go back to work when they should be enjoying retirement. For that reason, I do everything I can to lower their investment risk and to help them take advantage of relatively safe investments that can produce a reliable income stream month after month, year after year.

As I am writing in 2021, the stock market is at all-time highs. In most parts of the country, the real estate market is at an all-time high.

Now is the perfect time to cash in some chips, to take some chips off the table, to take some of your money out of the stock market casino and out of the real estate casino and put some of your money into safe investments that are guaranteed to produce reliable income for the rest of your life.

CHAPTER SIX

HOW MY POWERFUL FOUR-BUCKET SYSTEM WORKS

Let's go deeper into how my four-bucket system works.

The Emergency Bucket

In your emergency bucket, you need to keep enough money in a savings or money market account (a liquid account) to take care of almost any emergency. This account should not be invested in anything—it should be available at a moment's notice.

For most people, I advise keeping **three to six months of your monthly expenses in this account**. However, some people may feel more comfortable have a year or two worth of expenses in this liquid account.

There are some exceptions. For example, if your house and cars are paid for and your children are grown and on their own, you may feel comfortable keeping a smaller amount of money in your emergency account. Also, if you have an outstanding health insurance plan that covers almost everything, it might be acceptable to have a little less in reserves in your emergency account.

However, if you have a large mortgage, have car payments to make and have children still living with you, it might be wise to keep a little more than three to six months of emergency expense money liquid.

In today's uncertain world, it is impossible to predict when someone might be laid off, be in a car accident, develop health problems or face some other emergency.

If you have any doubt about how much money you should keep in emergency funds, meet with a skilled financial advisor and obtain expert, unbiased advice.

The peace of mind this could provide you is priceless.

The Long-Term Bucket

Your long-term investment bucket should be filled with medium to long-term investments. These can include but are not limited to: stocks, ETFs, mutual funds, bonds, and/or real estate.

Other long-term investments are: a business you build that you could eventually sell, a tax-deferred long-term annuity, a 401K, an IRA or Roth IRA, or a cash value life insurance plan such as a whole life policy or a universal life policy.

While an insurance policy is not technically an investment, **it is possible to build up a cash value of hundreds of thousands of dollars or even $1 million or more in certain insurance policies.** Please note that this is not the life insurance policy's face value (or insurance value). The policy's face value or insurance value is always several times larger than the cash value of the policy.

Stocks and Stock Dividends

Historically, stocks have increased an average of around 10 to 11% per year (source: https://www.investopedia.com/ask/answers/042415/what-average-annual-return-sp-500.asp)

This is based on the S&P index. Other indices return slightly less or slightly more over long periods of time.

Keep in mind that these are averages. During some years, the index will lose value (in some cases, a lot of value). During other years, the index will vastly out-perform its historical average. Due to the volatile nature of the stock market, you should plan on being a long-term investor.

While stocks have historically been the best-performing asset class (significantly out-performing real estate and bonds), one of the problems for retirees is that many stocks do not produce a very large income stream and many stocks (especially growth stocks and high technology stocks) pay no dividends.

Planning for income during retirement is very different than investment planning when you are younger. When you are young and have time on your side, you can handle a significant loss because you have years or even decades for the stock market to recover. Also, you don't need to rely much on dividends because you have a full-time job to generate the income you need.

When you are older, you may not have the time to wait for the stock market to recover from a significant loss. Also, when you are retired, you need investment income to replace the income your job previously generated. Unless you have a very large stock portfolio, it is unlikely that stock dividends alone will generate all the income you need.

For the above reasons, as many people approach retirement, they decide to take some stock market risk off the table, lock in their gains and shift more of their money into safer investments that generate a substantial passive income stream.

What happens when some clients go to a broker and say, "**I want a more conservative portfolio**"? In some cases, the broker will reduce the client's stock holdings and will move more money into bonds. Not all brokers are alike, but this is still a commonly followed practice.

The challenge for investors is that bonds can also decline in value. While bonds are not as volatile as stocks, **when interest rates rise, bonds typically lose value.**

Currently, we are at historically low interest rates. However, since interest rates have NEVER stayed low forever, and since they have been very low for over a decade, bond rates may likely rise in the future and perhaps in the near future.

As previously stated, when interest rates rise, bond prices usually fall. This means that any bonds you own could be worth LESS than you paid for them. Since many experts are now predicting a rise in interest rates (and home mortgage rates have already increased), you should be very cautious about buying bonds at this time.

Real Estate as a Long-Term Investment

According to the Case-Shiller Housing Index, the average annualized rate of return for housing increased 3.7% between 1928 and 2013 (source: https://www.investopedia.com/ask/answers/052015/which-has-performed-better-historically-stock-market-or-real-estate.asp)

Over long periods, real estate can be an outstanding investment. However, **real estate is one of the most illiquid investments of all**.

You can sell most stocks or mutual funds in one minute or less. It can take weeks, months and sometimes over one year to sell some real estate, depending on the type of real estate and the market.

Real estate is also labor-intensive and expense intensive. If you invest in a rental house, for example, you have to be prepared to deal with "tenants, termites and toilets."

Rent can provide a good income stream, but rent is not guaranteed. During the coronavirus pandemic, there was a national moratorium on evictions. Some tenants stayed in their houses or apartments for many months without paying any rent and there was absolutely nothing the landlord could do to evict them.

During this time of receiving no rental income, landlords still had to pay their mortgages, property taxes, insurance and all of their maintenance expenses. With no income coming in from rent and a constant outlay of expenses, a number of landlords ran out of money to pay their mortgages, were foreclosed upon and lost their properties.

Even during good times, you have to plan for vacancies and repairs and both of these have a negative impact on your income.

Real estate is also very cyclical and goes through many boom and bust cycles. In certain cities and towns, real estate hardly rises in value (witness Detroit and many small towns in the Midwest).

Real Estate may fail to rise in price during a bust cycle or even decline in value for many years. During these years, you still have to keep paying your mortgage, taxes, insurance and maintenance costs.

When a major employer closes in a city or town, employment falls, and many people leave to seek a job elsewhere. That can lead to a surplus of houses, rising vacancies and even abandoned houses.

In Detroit alone, there were thousands of abandoned homes and a number of them were left to rot, were torn down, or were even set on fire by vandals.

In smaller industrial towns in Ohio and other states where a city depends on one major factory, real estate prices can fall precipitously when that factory shuts down.

While real estate can be a good investment long-term, due to its boom and bust cycles and its labor-intensive and expense-intensive nature, it can be one of the most challenging investments of all for a retired person.

Owning a Business as a Long-term Investment

Entrepreneurs and business owners have created great wealth. I salute entrepreneurs and business owners and I have had many of them as clients.

I love to see people start new businesses. However, you have to be realistic about your chances of success.

What percentage of new businesses succeed? "According to data from the **Bureau of Labor Statistics**, as reported by Fundera, approximately 20 percent of small businesses fail within the first year. By the end of the second year, 30 percent of businesses will have failed. By the end of the fifth year, about half will have failed. And **by the end of the decade, only 30 percent of businesses will remain**—a 70 percent failure rate. (Source: https://www.entrepreneur.com/article/361350#:~:text=According%20to%20data%20from%20the,about%20half%20will%20have%20failed)

It is sporadic that an entrepreneur can build a business quickly and sell it for a significant profit. In most cases, it takes many years to grow a business into a successful enterprise.

If you are one of the 30% of entrepreneurs whose business is still around after 10 years and is successful, you deserve great respect. You put a lot of blood, sweat, tears and money into growing that business.

Due to all of the time and energy, it takes to run a business, to keep track of income and expenses and inventory, and to hire and train employees, few retirees want to put in all the effort required to continue running that business.

Therefore, they attempt to sell the business. With the proceeds of the business sale, the retiree can invest in high-quality, safe investments that will produce a reliable income stream to support the retiree for the rest of their life.

HOW TAXES ERODE YOUR WEALTH

Unless you are very poor, taxes will erode your wealth every single year of your adult life. A tax-deferred annuity can help you deal with the challenges posed by taxation.

In addition, a tax-deferred annuity can be converted to an income stream that can provide you with a lifetime income. Notice that I referred to annuities as "**tax-deferred**" rather than **tax-free**. The distinction is important.

As your wealth grows in an annuity, whether through interest paid or credits earned in an equity-linked annuity, you pay no current taxes. If you purchased an annuity at **age 25** and let it grow until **age 65**, your wealth could grow for 40 years, being totally untaxed.

When you start taking distributions (an income stream) from your annuity, you will owe taxes only on the part of the distribution that represents a gain. The portion of your monthly payment that is a return of principal is totally untaxed.

Why are tax-deferred vehicles so powerful in building wealth? Imagine that you took $1 and doubled it every year for twenty years without paying taxes along the way. How much money would you have at the end of those 20 years period? **$1,048,576**.

However, if you paid taxes every year on your earnings and were in the 35% tax bracket at the end of twenty years, you will be left with only **$22,370.66**. That's a whopping **$1,026,205** lost due to the wealth-eroding effects of annual taxation.

The table below illustrates the above example. Please take a look at how $1 doubled every year for twenty years rises in value when it is taxed every year and when it is not taxed?

The first column shows how your wealth grows if you pay no current taxes (tax-deferral) and the second column shows how paying a 35% tax on your earnings every year erodes that wealth.

	NO CURRENT TAX	35% TAX BRACKET
YEAR 1	$1.00	$1.00
YEAR 2	$2.00	$1.65
YEAR 3	$4.00	$2.72
YEAR 4	$8.00	$4.49
YEAR 5	$16.00	$7.41
YEAR 6	$32.00	$12.23
YEAR 7	$64.00	$20.18
YEAR 8	$128.00	$33.00
YEAR 9	$256.00	$54.94
YEAR 10	$512.00	$90.65
YEAR 11	$1,024.00	$149.57
YEAR 12	$2,048.00	$246.79
YEAR 13	$4,096.00	$407.20
YEAR 14	$8,192.00	$671.88
YEAR 15	$16,384.00	$1,108.60
YEAR 16	$32,768.00	$1,829.19
YEAR 17	$65,536.00	$3,018.17
YEAR 18	$131,072.00	$4,979.97
YEAR 19	$262,144.00	$8,216.96
YEAR 20	$524,288.00	$13,557.98
YEAR 21	$1,048,576.00	$22,370.66

As you can see, taxes can take a tremendous bite out of your gains. Also, the above chart does not even factor in **state taxes**, which in a state like California **can be more than 10% per year** on top of your federal tax rate.

When you invest using a tax-deferred investment vehicle, you can legally avoid paying taxes on your gains year after year for decades. Taxes will be owed only when you take money out of your account, sell investments or annuitize your annuity.

If you wait to take money out until you are retired, your total annual income should be less and you may very well be in a lower tax bracket.

Add the benefits up: you avoided paying annual taxes on your gains for many, many years and when you do take money out, if you are retired and in a lower tax bracket, **you will probably pay** fewer **taxes on those gains**. THAT is a winning combination.

DO YOU WANT TO PAY TAXES ON THE SEED OR THE HARVEST?

By using 401Ks, IRAs, Roth IRAs, pensions and annuities, you can defer paying taxes until you start taking income. The exception is distributions from Roth IRAs, which are totally tax-free because you don't get the tax deduction upfront as most people do on traditional IRAs.

I often recommend **Roth IRAs** for younger people. With a Roth IRA, your retirement funds can build up tax-free for decades and you can take out all of the money tax-free in retirement. It does not get any better than that.

With a Roth IRA, you pay taxes on the seed and reap tax-free benefits on the harvest. However, there are limitations. For example, if you are married and filing jointly, or if your income is over $208,000 for a married couple or $140,000 for single filers in 2021, you cannot contribute to a Roth IRA.

Please note tax rates and amounts you can contribute to your IRAs, 401K's and other retirement programs change on a regular basis. Feel free to contact me and I will be happy to provide you with the latest tax rates and I will show you the best ways to contribute to your retirement accounts. As both a CPA and PFS (Personal Financial Specialist), I keep up with all of the tax code changes and I can provide you with the high-quality information you need. With traditional IRAs and 401Ks, most people get the tax benefit now (a reduction in their taxable income) but pay taxes later when income is withdrawn. For example, if you contributed $10,000 a year for twenty years into your 401K at work, your taxable income each year will be reduced by $10,000. Over a twenty-year period, you will have a $200,000 reduction in reportable income.

If your account grows to $500,000 by the time you retire, you will pay taxes on whatever portion of that $500,000 you withdraw each year. So, you get the tax benefit now and pay for it later.

However, if instead, you had been making contributions to a Roth IRA each year, your taxable income would not have been reduced during the 20-year period. If your Roth IRA grew to the same $500,000 upon your retirement (assuming you are at least 59 ½ years old and had your Roth IRA for at least five years), **then you could withdraw the entire $500,000 or any portion of it totally tax-free in retirement.**

Another very nice benefit of a Roth IRA is that you can withdraw contributions you have made into the Roth IRA at any time, penalty-free and tax-free.

Cash-Value Life Insurance.

An additional powerful wealth-creation solution for income earners is **cash-value life insurance**. With cash-value life insurance, you can build up tremendous value within your insurance policy.

Some people have built up cash values within these insurance policies of $5 million to $10 million or even more. Even if you only build up to $50,000 or $100,000 cash-value in your insurance policy, that is much better than owning an insurance policy with no cash value.

Once you have built up a certain cash value in your policy, you can borrow out money at a very low-interest rate.

The Power and Safety of the Income Bucket

Your goal is to fill your **Income Bucket** with investments that will provide you with an income that is guaranteed for life.

How much income do you need in retirement? Start first by looking at your **projected living expenses** in retirement and look at what your **projected income in retirement** is expected to be. Then, notice the size of the gap between those two figures. Is there a shortfall or a surplus?

For example, if your expenses in retirement are projected to be **$5,000 a month** and your Social Security and other projected income is expected to total **$2,400 a month**. Your shortfall is **$2,600** per month.

A high-quality annuity is one of the only investment vehicles that could provide you with a guaranteed $2,600 or more per month for the rest of your life.

As I have written about earlier in the book, there are many different types of annuities. I prefer an indexed annuity with a return linked to but not directly invested in the stock market index (such as the S&P 500).

I also like indexed annuities because the best ones can have lower fees than some other types of annuities. In addition, indexed annuities protect your principal if the stock market declines. Even if a major stock market index falls by 30% or more in one year (as it sometimes has) as long as you do not cash in your annuity early, your annuity will suffer NO losses in value.

Additionally, when you start taking income from your annuity (a process called Annuitization or lifetime income), your income stream is guaranteed for life. With certain types of annuities or with bonus features called "annuity riders," your income stream can also be guaranteed to go up each year—even if the stock market declines. Please note that there may be a small extra charge for this inflation protection feature.

How much of your retirement savings should be invested in annuities? I usually advise my clients to put in enough money to guarantee that they will have all of the income they need to pay all of their monthly bills in retirement.

Once that need is met, you can invest your remaining funds in other investment vehicles depending on your time frame and risk tolerance.

An annuity is the only investment or savings vehicle that provides what I call **longevity credits**. Longevity credits will continue to provide you with a monthly income stream even if the account value goes down to zero.

Even if you live to 120 (and I hope you do), an annuity will continue to provide you with a lifetime safe income.

My clients Mike and Barbara Jones came to see me in 2007. Mike had just retired and I helped him put a plan together to guarantee his and Barbara's retirement security.

Their **concerns** were as follows:

1. To never run out of money in retirement.

2. They also wanted to keep up with inflation.
3. To leave a legacy for their two children.
4. To provide for Long Term Care costs as they did not want to burden their kids.

We set an **Income Annuity** to provide an income stream to cover all their expenses for both of their lives while keeping up with inflation.

I helped them acquire high-quality insurance policies for pennies on the dollar. These policies greatly increased the value of their estate and the proceeds will be income tax-free for the benefit of their two children.

We also put aside funds to provide both of them with long-term care. The policies have the potential to pay out a multiple of what they paid in and the benefits will be received tax-free.

I addressed all of their financial concerns in setting up their financial plan. They never stressed during the stock market crash of 2008 and 2009 because they lost no money. Despite the stock market crash and the ensuing Great Recession, the monthly income from their annuities arrived on time and in full every 30 days.

They are fortunate that neither of them has needed long-term care so far. Their health is holding up well. Perhaps that is because they are living a relatively stress-free life and are really enjoying their retirement.

Since their children will be totally taken care of by their insurance policies, they have no guilt about spending their hard-earned money on enjoying themselves in retirement. Mike and Barbara still call and thank me for what we have been able to provide for them. They tell me they enjoy traveling, seeing their grandkids and pursuing their favorite hobbies. Nothing gives me more pleasure than witnessing good people thoroughly enjoying their hard-earned retirement. Solid financial planning made this all possible.

I could write an entire second book full of success stories like this.

Mike and Barbara had all of their Financial Buckets full of suitable savings vehicles, investment vehicles, annuities and insurance products. They are middle-class, not rich (although sometimes they tell me that they feel rich.).

You do NOT have to be rich to achieve financial peace of mind IF you do the right kind of financial planning with the funds you have.

Make sure you have a **liquidity bucket** for emergencies and have a properly designed **long-term bucket** to keep up with inflation and secure lifetime income from the most reliable sources possible.

The best annuities are issued by billion-dollar life insurance companies that are required by law to have assets that can pay out all claims and fulfill all promised income streams. However, not all annuities are created equal. Therefore, you need to work with an annuity expert who can help you select the very best annuity or annuities for your situation.

The Love You Leave with Your Legacy Bucket

With your **Legacy Bucket**, you can take care of the next generation, your loved ones and your favorite charities. In addition, you want to fill your Legacy Bucket with high-quality, safe longer-term investments and insurance products.

For a variety of reasons, **life insurance** is a perfect choice for your Legacy Bucket. First, because the proceeds to the beneficiary **are income tax-free**. Second, if structured and appropriately held, the proceeds can also be **estate tax-free**. Third, with your Legacy Bucket filled with life insurance, which is guaranteed to pay out a certain sum of money (there is no market risk) all of your beneficiaries will be financially provided for. You can then spend all of your life savings on enjoying your life in retirement without guilt.

Can you imagine how your kids will feel when they realize that **Mom and Dad loved them so much they planned ahead and left them with a sizeable Tax-Free inheritance?**

The funds you leave your children with life insurance can be used to pay for or buy anything. Your spouse, children, or other loved ones can use the proceeds from a life insurance policy to buy a new car, put a down payment on a house or maybe even buy a house and completely pay it off. They can use the funds to go to the college of their choice or go to law school or medical school or pay off college loans. The proceeds from a life insurance policy can be used to save for retirement or fund a nest egg. They can be used to buy new furniture, remodel the house, or travel worldwide. Whatever they do with these funds, they can use them to reduce or eliminate debt, reduce financial stress, and truly enjoy life. And your loved ones will ALWAYS remember you for the loving gift of this financial help that you provided them. This is your Financial Legacy.

Another legacy you can leave your children and loved ones is to **be a role model** by living your life to the fullest and including them. In addition to the financial resources, you leave them, you will also be leaving them precious memories that they will cherish for the rest of their life.

CHAPTER SEVEN

10 BIG MISTAKES TO AVOID IN RETIREMENT PLANNING

Retirement should be an exciting and relatively stress-free time in your life—and it can be. By taking a little time to develop your retirement plan now and avoiding the pitfalls discussed earlier in this book, you can enter this chapter of your life with a high level of confidence and excitement.

1. Not Understanding Cash Flow Needs:

This is the first big mistake you MUST avoid if you want to live a happy and fulfilled retirement.

So why exactly is it so important to understand your cash flow needs? From a financial planner's perspective, if you don't know what your annual expenses, debts, and estimated taxes are going to be in retirement, it is nearly impossible to figure out if you have accumulated enough assets and have a sufficient income flow to pay these bills and also to have some money left over to enjoy life.

TIP: *over several months, write down everything you spend money on. It is important to do this over a several-month periods because some months will have MUCH larger expenses due to periodic payments that must be made for things such as auto insurance, property taxes, medical bills, etc. There are also online services you can sign up for that you can use to track all expenses and expenditures.*

Then, after four or so months, total up all the money you spent. You might be shocked at how much it is and just by looking at the list, you might gain valuable insights as to which expenses can be eliminated or greatly reduced.

2. Failing to Factor in Inflation:

Let's say that you tracked all of your expenses for one year in the above exercise (or tracked all of your expenses for four months and multiplied that by 3 to get an estimate of the annual expenses). Let's say that your living expenses are $85,000 per year. Guess what? That number is going to be **higher** every year in the future due to the effects of inflation.

As I am writing this in June of 2021, the news is reporting that the year over year inflation from May 2020 to May 2021 was 5%. When you are planning your retirement, you must factor in impact of inflation. This simply means that things are going to cost more in the future, and therefore you will require more cash flow to maintain the same lifestyle you have today.

In the late 1970s and early 1980s, inflation spiked upwards in the USA. In 1980, inflation hit 13.5%. (source: https://www.in2013dollars.com/inflation-rate-in-1980#:~:text=The%20inflation%20rate%20in%201980,CPI%20in%201980%20was%2082.40.)

As shocking as that was, many experts believe we could once again have such a rate of inflation. From the mid-1970s to the mid-1980s, prices for basic goods doubled. Such price increases remind us of the fact that we not only need to keep up with inflation but to outpace it.

Inflation has destroyed the economies of countries in Africa and South America and Germany in the past and it is still a problem in some countries today. So, we certainly are not immune to the possibility that inflation could have a big negative impact on our economy. Already, we are forced to rent instead of buy. Others who cannot even afford the rapidly rising rents have been left homeless and have contributed to the massive homeless problem we have today.

In the last months of the Trump administration and in the early months of the Biden administration, our country has been flooded with trillions of dollars of "stimulus" money to help us recover from the corona virus pandemic. This unprecedented amount of stimulus money is one of the factors fueling the current rise in inflation.

We can fight the inflation dragon with carefully selected investments that offer inflation protection and safety. There are a number of choices in this area and to cover them would take many more chapters. If you are interested in getting inflation protection for your savings and investments, contact us and discuss which options are best for you and your family.

3. Not Adjusting Your Investment Strategy Well Before Retirement:

Are you still investing the same amount in your 401k or IRA as you were ten or twenty years ago? The odds are that you had a fairly aggressive risk tolerance when you began investing, as you figured you had a decade or longer until retirement. Well, if you are reading this, you are probably within a few years of retiring (or may even be retired) and it is time to reexamine that youthful investment strategy.

One major drop in the market could set your retirement date back several years—or even a decade.

4. The Dangers of Chasing Investment Returns:

Are you chasing investment returns? Are you trying to find the next hot stock or hot mutual fund? Are you looking at or investing in Bitcoin or other volatile cryptocurrencies?

Retirement isn't the time to begin day trading your retirement account or to begin chasing the hot stock of the day. If you feel you must hit home runs (get big stock market returns) to either impress your buddies or maintain your lifestyle, you may be putting your entire retirement in jeopardy. If you really have the urge to speculate and you have enough assets, consider setting up a separate "play" account.

Don't gamble with your retirement nest egg. If you feel that you absolutely must speculate, do so only with a tiny amount of play money. Keep your serious money, your retirement money, in safe and secure investments.

Remember my Uncle Joe, who invested his life savings in the stock market just before the dot com bubble crashed around the year 2000. He and his broker were chasing returns instead of looking for reliable income. My Uncle Joe paid a terrible price for that.

During the dot com bubble crash, which was only about 21 years ago, many people lost 40% to 50% of their life savings and some lost even more.

Your **investment mindset** should be completely different in retirement than it was when you were younger. Young people are still in the **accumulation phase** where they should focus on accumulating wealth.

In retirement, however, you are in the **distribution phase.** During this phase of your investment life, your focus needs to be on **wisely distributing and using the assets you have accumulated so that you can have a steady source of income WITHOUT working.**

If you have planned your financial life wisely, there is absolutely no need to take big risks by chasing returns in retirement. You should have all the money and assets you need to enjoy a happy and fulfilled retirement.

5. Retiring With Too Much Debt:

While entering retirement debt-free is always the best scenario, but it isn't uncommon for folks to retire with a mortgage on their primary residence and perhaps a little credit card debt. What you want to be careful about is retiring with too much debt. Constantly worrying about draining your retirement accounts to keep up with mortgage payments or credit card bills or car payments isn't an enjoyable way to spend your retirement.

Therefore, in the decade before they retire, I advise all of my clients to do everything they can do to pay down as much debt as possible. A number of my clients have even been able to pay off their home mortgage before they retire.

6. Failing to Consider Health-Related Costs:

There are two items to consider here:

If you are retiring early (before the age of sixty-five or Medicare eligibility), it is a good idea to shop around for good health insurance and get cost estimates. **Do not just look for the cheapest health insurance plan.** Some health insurance plans are very low cost because they have very high deductibles (meaning you pay a much higher percentage of every health care bill) and offer far fewer benefits.

As many people have learned to their dismay, a cheap health insurance plan can often cost you much MORE in the long run.

When you learn the cost of your health insurance plan, make sure to include it in your budget. You want to make sure you can always pay the monthly premium on your health insurance because if you let your health insurance lapse and get ill or get into an accident, the financial costs can be devastating.

Prior to transitioning into retirement, **you need also to understand what kind of financial impact a** significant **health issue or long-term care illness could have on your retirement assets.**

Health care costs can be as much as $250,000 or more in the course of your retirement. If you are one of the millions of Americans who end up needing long-term care, that could cost you $10,000 a month or much more depending on what part of the country you are living in and the level of care you need. In some facilities, long-term care costs are more than $15,000 per month, and Medicare does NOT cover it.

TIP**: Make sure to budget for Medicare Supplement Insurance and Prescription Drug Coverage in your monthly cash flow (unless you are signing up for a Medicare Advantage Plan). For added peace of mind and financial security, consider exploring long-term care insurance to help cover the cost of assisted living or skilled nursing care. I urge* *people to look into Asset Based Long Term Care, introduced back in 2010 by the Pension Protection Act. If you do not buy insurance from an insurance company, realize that you are* ***self-insuring*.*

In many cases, **self-insurance is the MOST expensive type of insurance of all** because you are subject to almost unlimited medical bills. Remember that medical bills are one of the leading causes of bankruptcy in America. You do not want to subject yourself to that kind of almost unlimited risk.

7. Not Understanding the Required Rate of Return Needed to Support Retirement Lifestyle:

Many would consider retiring with $1,000,000 in retirement assets pretty nice, but if you require $100,000 per year in distributions to cover your annual expenses and lifestyle, then you might want to rethink retirement or adjust your budget.

If you do not have another source of income and have to withdraw $100K a year to live on, after 10 short years, you will be out of money.

$100K per year out of a $1 million nest egg is a 10% withdrawal rate without figuring in taxes. Remember that if you are taking this money out of a regular IRA or 401(K) or pension plan, in most cases, full taxes will be owed.

You cannot count on the stock market to bail you out. In some cases, after a severe stock market crash, it can take 10 years or longer for the stock market to recover to where it had been. If you are withdrawing money from your stock market account during this 10-year slump, there is a good probability that you will never recover from that stock market crash.

There are ways to generate moderate returns **safely** in today's market; however, you need to understand in advance what is required to sustain your assets throughout retirement.

I can help you live the retirement lifestyle you want with a guaranteed lifetime income. This is income you can never out-live, even if you live to be 120 or older. You can take enjoyable vacations to your favorite spots in the world. So you can take cruises, visit grandkids and go to nice restaurants and enjoy entertainment. You can enjoy your favorite hobbies. You can have this kind of lifestyle without taking unnecessary risks IF you have the right investments.

8. Failing to Develop a Proper Distribution Strategy:

You have spent a lifetime saving up for retirement; now how exactly do you start taking money from your various accounts? From which account should you take money first, second, or third?

It is a confusing question for many people. One of the reasons for the confusion is because some people own a wide variety of assets and retirement accounts: investment real estate, stocks, mutual funds, ETFs, corporate bonds and muni bonds, bond funds, 401ks, Roth 401ks, IRAs, Roth IRAs, pension plans, fixed annuities, variable annuities, 403 (b) annuities, CDs, cash-value life insurance plans, cash savings accounts and more.

Prior to moving into retirement, you need to have a game plan set in place for **how** and **when** you will take distributions from the various investments and assets you own. It would be best if you had a plan for when and how you will begin taking distributions from Social Security, pensions, 401K programs, IRAs and other retirement programs.

Finally, you need to decide if you are going to work and if so, what kind of work will you do and will it be full-time, part-time or seasonal?

As you can see, there are many moving parts here and **many complex decisions must be made properly to ensure that your money lasts as long as you do.**

Many of these decisions have income tax implications. Using my background and expertise as a Certified Public Accountant, I can help make sure that you are receiving your retirement income in the most tax-efficient way possible.

9. Not Understanding the Rules Regarding Withdrawals from 401ks, IRAs, Pensions and Annuities:

What do you do with that 401k once you retire? Should you transfer it to a "rollover" IRA or take a lump-sum distribution? Making the wrong decision can cost you thousands to tens of thousands of dollars or more in extra taxes—a fate you want to avoid.

Did you know that the IRS previously required you to take distributions from your IRA once you reach age 70 ½? These are called RMDs or Required Minimum Distributions. The age was changed to 72 during the coronavirus pandemic. However, now that the pandemic seems to be under control and maybe drawing to a close will the IRS change the age for RMDs back to 70 ½?

As you can see, **paying attention to all of these details in the constantly changing tax code takes a lot of time, attention and energy**. That is my job. I keep up with all of these many details in the ever-changing tax code and in retirement income planning so that you do not have to. YOUR job is to enjoy your retirement.

How about your pension or other retirement plans? In some cases, you have a choice between a 100% joint and survivor option, a straight life option, or a lump sum option. This is a complex decision. Seek the help and guidance of a skilled retirement planning advisor to make sure that you make the right choice.

You should always do what is best for you, your situation and your family.

10. Failing to Understand Long-Term Strategy and Making Decisions Out of Fear:

To be able to enjoy a successful retirement, you must have a well-thought-out game plan. But, do you really understand how your cash flow needs and investment strategy are related and intertwined?

Do you have a strategy that enables you to make **smart decisions** rather than emotional decisions?

Your retirement plan and retirement income plan should both be flexible. As times change and your needs change, you should review your retirement plan and customize it to meet your needs best. A retirement plan should not be poured into concrete.

If you avoid the mistakes discussed in this chapter and work with a skilled and knowledgeable financial advisor, you will be able to retire with **confidence** and **full peace of mind**. That is what I try to help all of my clients do, which is my wish for you.

CONCLUSION

Retirement isn't something to fear or dread—it's the start of a whole new chapter of your life with levels of freedom that you've probably never experienced before.

Hopefully, this book has provided you with insights on effective retirement planning that you can use to enjoy a more financially secure retirement. My goal is to help my clients safely maximize their income in retirement and keep their taxes as low as possible.

To live a happy, successful and fulfilled retirement, you must prepare in many different ways: physically, mentally, emotionally and financially.

Many people wonder what they will be doing during retirement. The short answer is that **retirement allows you to do almost anything that you want to do.**

Of course, you have to be physically able to do it. Traveling, playing golf, tennis and others sports, fishing and playing with your grandchildren: all of this takes physical energy and stamina.

For that reason, you want to maintain a healthy weight, eat a healthy diet, quit smoking if you smoke, limit drinking, get lots of exercises, manage stress and get a good night's sleep.

In retirement, at first, it may seem like you have all the time in the world. However, your schedule will quickly fill up with friends and family, social events, hobbies and recreational activities, travel and an occasional trip to the doctor. Some of my clients tell me they are as busy in retirement as they were when they were working.

Make sure that in all of that activity, you are following your dreams and making the most of your freedom.

Work, although it brings in money, can be stressful and tiresome. So, imagine retirement as a much-needed vacation that can, depending on your needs and interests, have periods of work or volunteer activity.

How to Keep Your Sense of Purpose in Retirement

Some people fear that in retirement, they might lose their sense of purpose in life. However, suppose you plan well for your retirement. In that case, you might find retirement more profoundly meaningful and purposeful than earlier periods of your life when you had to focus on climbing the career ladder, earning money, paying bills, etc.

When we are younger, we do a lot of things because we are expected to do them by our parents or peers. We work to pay the bills and "keep up with the Joneses" or to try to get ahead of the Joneses.

In retirement, you finally have the freedom to do what YOU want to do. So make the most of this opportunity.

Some people worry that they will have to look for ways to fill up their days in retirement. Based on my work with my clients, that has not been their experience. You need to live each day to the fullest. **Pursue your dreams.** Do all of those things that you did not have the time or the money to pursue when you were younger.

In retirement, our jobs do not dictate who we are or what we do. In retirement, you can keep the schedule YOU want (no more 9 to 5.), spend time with the people YOU want to spend time with and do the things YOU want to do.

In retirement, you can really focus on enjoying life and being the best that you can be.

In order to avoid idleness, make a schedule or develop a plan for doing the things you really want to do. Don't tell yourself, "I'll get around to it someday." We all have a tendency to procrastinate.

Without a written plan and a timetable, that trip to Paris might never happen. Without a written plan and a timetable, that novel you always planned to write might never get written. Without a **written plan** and a **schedule**, your dreams of A, B and C might never happen.

Start by writing down a list of your **favorite activities**: visiting friends and family (including grandchildren), your favorite hobbies, recreational activities and sports and maybe try out a new hobby that might become your favorite hobby. Travel: where do you and your spouse MOST want to go and when will you go there?

Also, remember the vital role that **spiritual activity** can play in living a happy and fulfilling retirement. Many retirees get more actively involved than ever with their church, temple, or house of worship. **Charity work** and **volunteerism** can also lead to deep fulfillment in retirement. Whatever you give with your time, attention, expertise and love can come back to you tenfold as you see how you are enriching the lives of others in your community.

Making new friends in retirement can be exciting and deeply rewarding. Making new friends in retirement can help you develop parts you did not know you had and is a great way to enjoy life as well. Your new friends, along with your existing friends, can help you on your journey through this new chapter of your life—retirement—and you can find meaning in life by supporting them.

In retirement, you will finally have the time to join clubs where you'll meet people with the same interests you have. In these clubs, you may develop a skill or even become an expert in a new area or an existing area of interest. Therefore, I suggest that you start looking for clubs and special interest groups before you actually retire to ease the transition into retirement and so that you will have an exciting schedule of things to do once you retire.

One strong area of interest for many people is **travel**. When you are young or middle-aged, you might not have the time or the money to pursue your travel dreams. However, many folks find that in retirement, they can finally not just pursue those travel dreams but actually live those dreams.

There are many travel clubs for people who love to travel or want to travel more. No matter where you want to travel to in the world, you will be able to find someone who has been there and who can share valuable travel tips, recommend great hotels and restaurants and experiences to have when you are in that city or that part of the world.

You might even find a great new friend or a couple to travel with and share your experiences with.

Imagine the joys and thrills of traveling around the world when you are retired. You can, in a sense, become a Citizen of the World. Some retirees even become Perpetual Travelers (PT's).

When you are retired, you can experience the world to the fullest without the worries you might have had when you were younger ("What is happening back at the office?" "Will our kids be interested in traveling to _________?").

Continue to Pay Attention to Finances in Retirement

Very few of us will retire with so much money that we can ignore our finances in retirement. Therefore, one of the most important calculations to do BEFORE you retire is to figure out how much monthly income you will need in retirement.

Usually, people need around 70% of their current income to maintain their lifestyle in retirement. For example, if you needed $10,000 a month prior to retirement to maintain your lifestyle, in retirement, you should plan on being able to generate about $7,000 a month in retirement income.

This is based on the assumption that your home mortgage is paid off and there are no other debts at the time of retirement. If you still have a home mortgage or credit card debt, or other debt, you will most likely need to generate MORE than 70% of your pre-retirement income to support your lifestyle.

How much money you will need each month in retirement depends on what activities you plan to pursue after you're retired. Some hobbies can be very expensive. Others are almost free. The most important thing to remember is to live on less than you earn and consistently save some money each month if at all possible.

To put everything you have learned in this book together with your pre-existing knowledge, you want to develop a comprehensive plan that addresses your unique situation of where you are now and where you want to go. Then, set your financial GPS so that you can live your chosen retirement lifestyle.

Analyze your existing financial resources and your earning capacity (if you choose to work part-time in retirement). Next, take a close look at what your money is invested in and at the characteristics and performance of your investments.

How risky are your investments? Are you protected from a stock market or real estate market crash? I always try to protect my clients from such risks or to limit the damage such crashes can inflict.

What has been the performance of your investments over time? Any money that you have left in the bank has likely underperformed every other asset class, especially once you figure in taxes and inflation.

Are your investments or savings providing you with an income that you cannot outlive? I always try to make sure that my clients have an income stream like this.

Look to see if there is a better and safer way to achieve your financial goals. For example, a study was done by Hartford investments that found: "Those who have planned for retirement are three times more likely to be confident that they will have sufficient income in retirement compared to those that have not planned." If you want to be financially confident in retirement, meet with a financial advisor now to start setting up a plan that will help guarantee that you can reach your financial goals.

Let me tell you about John and Mary Miller. John worked as an executive for a large company and Mary was a homemaker who worked hard to raise happy and healthy children. They had built up a substantial net worth and were concerned about the impact of estate taxes. They wondered about the most efficient to transfer assets to their three children.

John had accumulated company stock which had gained tremendously in value and he also had a very large 401(K) from his previous employer. John also had a large pension. Between his and Mary's Social Security income and other income, they did not need John's 401(K) income.

At age 70 ½, John was forced to take his required minimum distribution from some of his retirement plans. This added to John's net worth. John and Mary's net worth was far in excess to the estate tax exemption had they not planned for this. John and Mary realized they would be facing a large estate tax bill.

Even though John had planned out his work life very successfully, he had not done a very good job with his estate planning. The only thing that John had for estate planning was an outdated will. He had no trust.

When they realized they would be facing a large estate tax bill, John and Mary contacted my office. We got to work on setting up a comprehensive financial plan and estate plan for John and Mary.

Sadly, John has now passed away. Due to the financial planning and estate planning I was able to do for them, everything is in order and his children are receiving a large inheritance tax-free.

The plan we set up saved the family over 2 million dollars in estate taxes and also avoided unnecessary probate on his assets and all the costs associated with probate. Before working with me, John handled all the family finances and his investments were scattered among different investments and were held by a variety of firms. Both he and Mary found that situation very confusing.

We organized John's investments and made it easy and simple for Mary to understand and handle the investments and savings vehicles. Mary is now enjoying financial peace of mind as her finances are all in order and are providing an income she can never outlive.

John and Mary took action and by doing so, they saved over 2 million dollars in unnecessary taxes and avoided a financial mess that Mary would have had to deal with.

The universe rewards people who take action. If you do not take action, nothing will change. But, if you take action, you could live the retirement of your dreams.

It would be my pleasure to help you plan for and then live the retirement of your dreams. Contact me by email at frank@frankguttacpa.com or go to my website Yoursaferetirementroadmap.com to set up a free no-obligation meeting to go over your retirement plans. We can meet in person or by phone or via zoom – whatever you prefer.

With my years of experience, with all the knowledge and training I have, I know that I can help you develop a Safe Retirement Roadmap that will get you safely to your destination of a secure, prosperous and happy retirement.

It's never too early to start planning for your retirement. The more you prepare, the better you prepare, the more financially secure, prosperous and happy you will be after you have retired.

Your retirement is too important to trust to luck. Remember that you have power over your life and you have the power to plan for the retirement of your dreams.

You and your spouse should make the most of your retirement and if you work with me, I will do everything possible to make sure that you do.

I look forward to working with you and to helping you achieve your retirement dreams.

Made in the USA
Columbia, SC
21 October 2024